Your
Flagship
Guide to
Successful
Leadership

SAM ADEYEMI

© 2022 Sam Adeyemi

For media interviews and bookings, contact David Ayodele

Info@SamAdeyemiGLC.com

1-404-937-4911 inside or outside of the United States

Customized signed orders are available from the author. Visit SamAdeyemi.com for more information.

Info@SamAdeyemiGLC.com

SamAdeyemi.com

Dr. Sam Adeyemi

@sam_adeyemi

SamAdeyemi

@TheSamAdeyemi

Sam Adeyemi TV

IAmSamAdeyemi

All rights reserved. No part of this book may be used or reproduced by any means, graphic, electronic, or mechanical, including photocopying, recording, taping or by any information storage retrieval system without the written permission of the author except in the case of brief quotations embodied in critical articles and reviews.

Acquisition Editor/Marketing Director Anne Bruce
Editorial Director Phyllis Jask
Art Director Brenda Hawkes
Covers by Flip Design Studio
Author photos by Herbert Kuper, Advanced Photo & Imaging, Atlanta, GA

ISBN-13: 979-884959421-7 (paperback)

DEAR LEADER,

I BELIEVE IN YOUR CAPACITY TO GROW YOUR INFLUENCE AND USE IT TO CHANGE OUR WORLD FOR GOOD. I DEDICATE THIS BOOK TO YOU.

CONTENTS

INTRODUCTION

Dear Leader,

Today you have a vision of who you want to become. I am here to help you achieve that vision.

Nobody makes it through life alone. Just as others were there to help me, I am here to help you. We learn from each other, encourage each other, inspire each other. By sharing our wisdom, we embolden others to continue. I am grateful for the help I had along my way, and I am here today to support you as a coach, a mentor, an author of this book, or in my certification training program based on this book. For information on how you or your team can participate in my High Impact Leadership Certification Program, please go to my website at SamAdeyemi.com and click on the High Impact Training Tab or email me at info@SamAdeyemiGLC.com with your inquiries.

It is through hard work, determination, and perseverance that you will accomplish your vision and become the leader you always imagined. Each one of us has inner strength and drive to succeed, we must dig deep within ourselves to tap into it. You may experience stumbling blocks, as I did in my youth growing up in Africa. As a young man, I thought I could only find success outside my impoverished home country. I thought a geographical change held all my answers. I endeavored to leave, but endured several disappointing mishaps in that process that kept me exactly where I was geographically. But a strange thing happened after my original plans fell apart. I experienced an internal transformation and a shift in my thinking. I dug deeper.

I tapped into my internal drive. I learned that past mistakes and failures only limit you if you let them. Geography does not matter. Location does not determine your future success. Success begins from inside you.

You see, leadership is a skill that anyone, anywhere can learn. You have the ability to influence others for the greater good, just as I am now influencing you to continue reading!

I wrote this book to guide you to become a successful leader. I share my experiences and humble beginnings as an example that even if you start with very little, you can still achieve personal growth and professional goals if your head and your heart are in the right place. Your self-image and how you value your self-worth are barometers for your future growth. You must believe in your own abilities in order to lead others to the same success you envision.

Trust the Process

I believe it is important that I convey two specific things. One, this book's content is evidence-based from a professional survey my team conducted over several months, on a global scale. The results of that survey are a critical part of the research that has gone into this timely and relevant leadership quest, including several of my keynote addresses. It was time for a fresh coat of paint on the leadership process, so my team and I stepped up, asked for and gathered your input, insights, suggestions, queries, and leadership priorities. Second, I hope that you will see yourself within the pages of this book because you are in it. I wrote this book for you. Do any of these statements below describe you?

- An aspiring entrepreneur
- A business leader ready for positive change

- A learning professional who wants to share new ideas with up-and-coming leaders
- An eager, emerging leader
- Someone ready for a second chance at leadership success after encountering a difficult experience or career disappointment
- A leader whose career could use a reboot
- A mid-level manager or supervisor whose career needs a fast, easy-to-learn program to implement leadership skill sets and strategies
- A virtual provider of leadership guidance and mentoring services
- Someone who simply wants to improve as a leader, influence more positively, and help others

I believe this book summarizes one-of-a-kind approaches to almost all areas of leadership and beyond. My work is based on the belief that leaders are nurtured and developed, supported and encouraged, and that within us all are leadership competencies that can be developed for mutual benefit, creating enormous human potential and higher-performing individuals and organizations that support them.

As you begin reading *Dear Leader*, I hope that you will find much of it thought-provoking and a practical resource you'll refer to time after time. It is my deepest desire that you will glean the most meaningful parts of this book and begin applying them as soon as possible. I am confident that when you do, you'll be leaving an indelible imprint on future leaders.

Ways to Use and Incorporate This Process Model

Lessons are often easier to use and apply when they are broken down into bite-sized chunks. I have simplified this leadership model into four main areas—all listed as 1, 2, 3, and 4. As you can see, they reside in their "lanes," and much like when you're driving on a highway, it is easy to get to your destination when you pick a lane and then when you are ready, you can change lanes or merge into other faster-moving traffic. Leadership growth is very much the same way.

A helpful tool for growth is seeing your path every day. To that end, I've created a visual graphic for the process model that you can copy and post where you can see it often. You can use it as a handout as a Learning Tool. It can be enlarged as a helpful poster. Individual pieces can become laminated bookmarks. Or I've had some readers actually tear it out of the book and tape it up near their desk or computer—but you don't have to do that. I am making it available for download on my website SamAdeyemi.com.

The process is simply an at-a-glance tool to help you see the bigger picture of what it takes to become the architect of your own leadership success story. As the saying goes, when you don't know where you're going, any road will take you there. Research shows us that when we see the bigger picture and envision what it takes to navigate our way there, our chances of success increase exponentially. Review each lane in the process below and check off the areas you have completed and those you'd like to expand upon. Some areas may not be necessary for your personalized leadership toolkit, so you can discard them. Others you may need to modify to fit your circumstances. The key is to have a process, work the process, adapt the parts that are best for you, and then trust that process to move you forward as you continue reading this book.

DR. SAM ADEYEMI

Successful Leadership Process Model

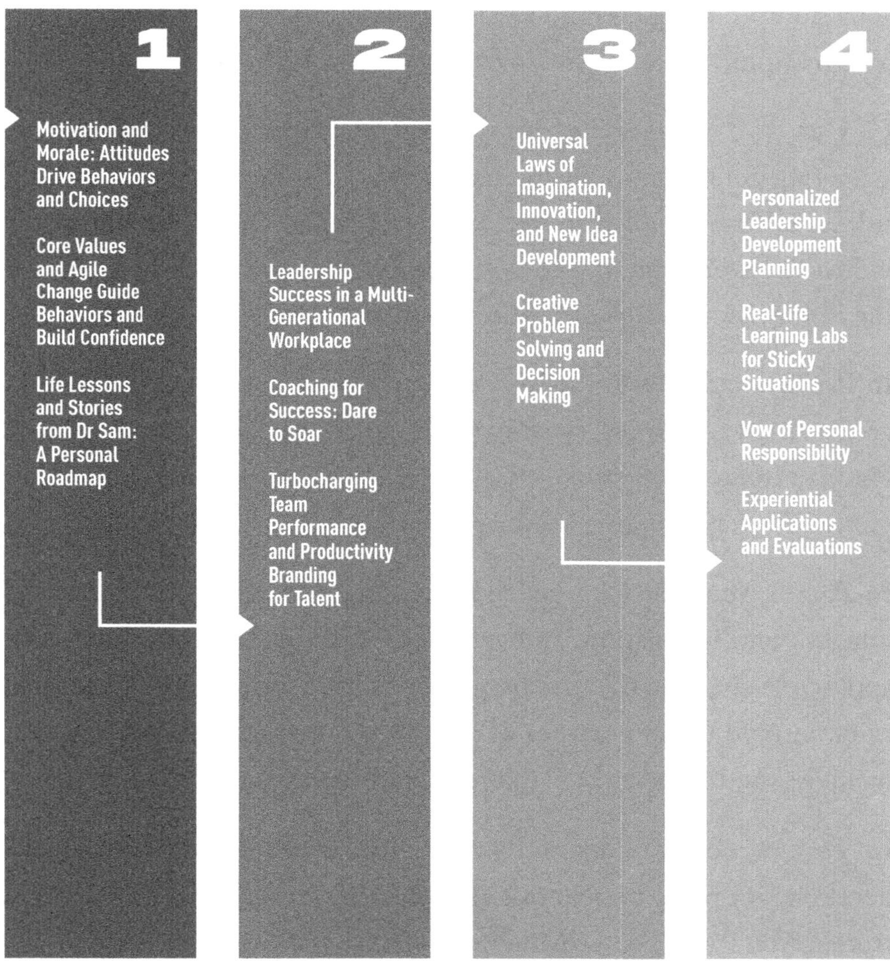

Inside This Book

By using the tools in this book, you can sharpen your skill set, activate your core values, become innovative and inspiring, make plans for your future development, and envision possibilities beyond your imagination. Here is a quick overview of what is to come.

In Part 1, I explain the importance of attitude and motivation, activating core values, and the importance of agile change for happier cultures. Here you'll discover how your values have the ability to influence others around you—for better or worse, so you will also learn the importance of applying your core values wisely.

In Part 2, we dive into the importance of communication in a multi-generational workforce, coaching, turbocharging teams, and branding for an entrepreneurial mindset, all paramount for successful leadership in today's ever-changing business world.

In Part 3, you will gain an understanding of the universal laws of imagination, innovation, and new idea development and how they apply to leadership. I'll also discuss new idea development, innovative thinking, and the importance of creative problem solving and decision making—and uncover how they go hand-in-hand.

In Part 4, you will learn how to map out individual employee development plans to help others around you write their own success stories. You'll see I've provided a roadmap for your ongoing success illustration and a helpful appendix for real-life sticky situations for in-the-moment-coaching.

Also within these pages, I will share my personal experiences using these tools, and how they have served me not only throughout my education and my career, but also throughout my life. It is my hope for you, dear leader, that you will take away from these stories the guidance you can begin using right away to chart and build a beautiful life in a way that is most successful for you.

I commend you for your focus and dedication to this flagship of successful leadership opportunity. Now let's get started.

—*Dr. Sam Adeyemi*

Part One

CHAPTER 1

Motivation and Morale: Attitudes Drive Behaviors and Choices

> **YOU CAN'T WAIT FOR INSPIRATION. YOU HAVE TO INVITE IT INTO YOUR LIFE.**
>
> —Dr. Sam Adeyemi

Early in my life, I thought of myself as somebody who wanted to go out into the world, and here I was a young man in the middle part of Nigeria. In fact, the town where I grew up did not even have a TV signal. Nobody had TV sets because there were no TV signals. One day a new family moved into the neighborhood. When we neighborhood kids visited the house and saw this box—their TV set—the kids in the house tried to explain what the box was and what it was for. We tried to conceptualize it but we didn't understand what they were describing. Seeing this strange box and what it represented sparked a curiosity in me. I was inspired and began to see myself as someone who wanted to explore the whole world, even though I didn't have a clear idea what the whole world was. There was more to life than I had ever known. To this day, I've never lost that vision of being a global person.

By the time I was through college, I found it difficult to get a job. I thought to myself, "I need to get out of Nigeria." I had the false notion that my problem was my environment, and I thought if I changed my environment, I would automatically change me. I endeavored to go to another country to seek my future, but it initially did not work out. I experienced a little bit of deprivation when I started out, much like many young people today. I was desperate to be successful in the sense of the traditional American Dream: a nice house, two cars, a good job, some extra money, a vacation here and there. And I was finding it difficult to put that together. I found out I had focused on myself too much. And I'm grateful for that wisdom now, but at the time not so much. I think I didn't succeed at first because I was lacking knowledge and action on basic principles and universal facts, which work everywhere on this planet, no matter where you are. One of those facts was it wasn't all about me; nobody succeeds all alone.

■■■

Every leader is unique. And every employee has his or her own individual personality. In addition to this, every organization has its own culture, or personality—some good, some not so good, some strong, some weak, some successful and happy, and others dysfunctional. As leaders, we all have strengths and talents and areas in which we can improve. When it comes to leadership and developing people, it is important to understand that these skills can, and should be, learned and honed over time. Leaders are not born with a gene that enables them to attract and retain superstar talent.

There is no denying that certain people have natural abilities and talents when it comes to leading a company or owning and running a business or influencing employees, and others have to work a little harder to develop those same skills. **But just as a bicycle can never attain the speed and performance of a Ferrari, a Ferrari will never be able to**

match the fuel economy offered by a bicycle. Each is unique, as are individual leaders and their approach to building work environments that will survive and thrive in the years ahead. Tapping into your own motivation and learning what motivates and inspires others is a mark of true leadership.

> **"MOTIVATION COMES FROM SHOWING PEOPLE YOU BELIEVE IN THEM."**
> —Herb Kelleher, Former Founder and Chairman of the Board, Southwest Airlines

Three Forms of Motivation and How They Work

Success is first about a state of being before it is a state of action. Motivation is intrinsic and comes from within you. One of the profound principles I discovered in my quest to experience a change in my circumstances is that success actually begins from the inside out. It must start within you before it manifests outwardly. You must initiate things in your heart and mind before you try to apply them in the physical world. Success begins in your heart. Knowing what your internal motivations are will guide your actions, and to sustain motivation, you need to address the "de-motivators." And once you have a solid grip on what motivates you, all you need to do is set your focus and intention for it. Then you'll be better positioned to influence others discover what motivates them.

The growing field of positive psychology shows that happiness doesn't magically arrive when you achieve what you believe is the definition of "success": having the right job, driving the right car, or living in the right house. It's the opposite—happiness drives success, and success comes from within you. Knowing what your intrinsic motivation is—fear, personal growth and development, desire, or fulfillment—gives you a foundation on which to build and models positive behavior for others to emulate.

Fear

Of all motivators, fear can be effective but it also has the potential to be the most damaging. Much as prehistoric people used to run from mortal danger, people today also use fear to keep us safe and out of harm's way, whether consciously or unconsciously. Fear can prevent you from pursuing your innermost dreams because your brain perceives any change from the status quo as harmful. Our brains want to keep us safe from the evils of the world and we do that by creating habits and routines. The irony is that inaction to pursue efforts outside of your normal routine and stay secure in the status quo can leave you stalled where you are—safe but unfulfilled. When the pain of fear is greater than the pleasure of achieving your ambition, you get stuck.

The hesitancy you may experience in pursuing your ambitions is much like the law of inertia: objects remain at rest unless acted upon by another force. Inertia is fear disguised as procrastination or safety or security. Your status in life will remain at a state of rest until you apply an internal force. That force can only come from within you. When you decide the pain of fear no longer holds you back, then you will be inspired to action.

On the other side of the argument, you can turn around fear to help push you to work harder to hit your goals. When you begin from examining your internal motivations, you are better equipped to act.

The balance shifts from the feeling of pain to the feeling of pleasure and happiness. The intersection of action is when your feeling of pleasure is stronger than your feeling of pain. It cycles back to what motivates you—is it the feeling of accomplishment, ownership, or recognition? Only you have the answers to your own motivation.

Fear can be an effective internal motivator if you channel it in the right direction. Determination to work beyond the pain of fear or whatever holds you back is a great motivator—reaching toward the good, the pleasurable is the greater endgame. Olympic athletes work beyond physical and mental fatigue because the feeling of accomplishment (winning) is greater than any physical challenge they encounter. The same can be said for any endeavor anyone in the history of time has accomplished. Motivation is born from chasing positive feelings that are greater than the pain of negative ones.

Are You Mindful of De-motivators?

Before you can bring real passion into your life and the workplace, you must first tear down the barriers that keep motivation out. These are called de-motivators. When you work to eliminate them, you mind the gap, as they say in Great Britain.

You may ask, "Minding the gap between what?" The answer is: Minding the gap between who you are and what you really want. Remember this key point: You cannot perform in a manner that is inconsistent with how you see yourself. By minding the gap between who you really are and what you really want in life, you can build a bridge to your greatest passion and dreams. It is then that you can become your most authentic and higher-performing self.

Beware of the Top 6 De-motivators:

1. **Fear.** Being afraid to make changes, or take risks, are strong de-motivators.
2. **Low Self-esteem.** Low self-esteem, or a lack of self-confidence, can derail motivation.
3. **Self-doubt.** You must believe in yourself if others are to believe in you and your vision.
4. **Complacency.** When complacency sets it, disaster strikes and the emotion necessary for motivation goes away.
5. **Bad Attitude.** A negative attitude is unacceptable. **A positive attitude drives passion—passion drives action—and action drives results.**
6. **Procrastination.** Whether it's laziness or uncertainty, procrastination postpones all motivation.

> **"MOTIVATED PEOPLE STAY THE COURSE."**
> —Dr. Sam Adeyemi

Incentives

Picture trying to motivate a stubborn mule. You can choose to motivate with force by using a stick, or you can motivate by dangling a tasty carrot in front of the mule's mouth, just out of its reach. In this context, fear is the stick, and incentive is the carrot. Humans much in the same way will reach for external motivations, such as money, rewards, praise, promotions, or other tangible rewards. These carrots of incentive are dangled in front of us to encourage us to complete our tasks. It's somewhat Pavlovian: we perform, we get a reward. But what happens once the mule reaches the carrot? What happens next? Does the mule expect to get more carrots each time it completes a task? Incentives have the potential to actually *undermine motivation* to perform: once we get into the habit of expecting a reward after each task, we keep expecting bigger and better rewards each time. When rewards fall short of the minimum, we lose our motivation to strive beyond mediocrity.

Today's incentives are tomorrow's expectations. Good leaders go beyond simple incentives and really tap into what motivates themselves and their teams. They provide rewards far beyond the tangible.

Personal Growth and Professional Development

Your personal motivation is the drive that moves you to do what you do, from getting up in the morning to exercise to going to work to make money to feeling acknowledged or recognized for a job well done. We are motivated to do what we believe is in our best interests. And that looks different for everybody.

When you look at personal growth and professional development as a motivator, you are shifting the way you think about your work, becoming more capable, and giving yourself a new meaning for working. Personal and professional growth are intrinsic motivators that tap into our tendency to seek out our best interests. We feel motivated to work hard when we feel empowered and accomplished, when we understand how our work adds value to our endeavors, and when we believe in the work we're accomplishing.

As a leader, you're a key influencer and play a role in how others around you perform—positively or negatively. But remember this: you can't motivate other people; you can only influence what they're motivated to do. You can act in ways that positively affect others' motivation to perform at higher levels. Working together to accomplish mutual goals can be a great source of meaningful purpose.

You can successfully help your team develop in both personal and professional capacities by providing the resources and tools they will need to do their jobs, including sharing critical knowledge, power, and training. Encouraging people to learn soft skills such as good communication, empathy, and emotional intelligence transcend workplace walls and help people lead more fulfilling lives.

> **"WHEN YOUR WORK IS A REFLECTION OF THE DESIRES OF YOUR HEART, YOU WILL PERFORM WITH EXHILARATION AND WITHOUT REGRET."**
>
> —Richard Chang, Author

Motivation Diagnostic —What Fires You Up and Why?

On a scale from one to four, with four being the highest rating and one being the lowest rating, assign a number to what motivates you to your highest level of performance.

Leadership caring about me as a person	4	3	2	1
Positive working relationships	4	3	2	1
Resources to get the job done	4	3	2	1
Leader's ability to make decisions	4	3	2	1
Leader who empowers others and walks the talk	4	3	2	1
Recognition of my efforts	4	3	2	1
Delegation of responsibility to me	4	3	2	1
Earned promotions	4	3	2	1
Customer interaction	4	3	2	1
Fair and equitable compensation	4	3	2	1
Teams who get along together	4	3	2	1
Honest praise and support	4	3	2	1
Constructive and corrective feedback	4	3	2	1
Coaching and career counseling	4	3	2	1
The result of a job well done	4	3	2	1
Being part of a successful team	4	3	2	1
Understanding expectations and boundaries	4	3	2	1
Security and safety	4	3	2	1
Up-to-date technology	4	3	2	1
(Something not on this list: add here):	4	3	2	1

Debrief: Take only the responses you graded a 4, or the highest rating. Choose the top three number 4s that mean the most to you. Circle only the top three.

Next, from the top three motivators you've selected, choose only one motivating factor that drives you to your highest level of performance and productivity. Yes, some responses may seem to have overlap, but choose only one that is most powerful to you. Put a star next to that response. There you have it. You've just uncovered your most important motivation.

Can you imagine how this could change your organization, team, or individual worker if you take time to administer this assessment to every person? You would immediately know what matters most to emerging leaders and when you have that information you can infuse more of it. For example, the response A job well done or Recognition of my efforts tells you as the leader precisely what that individual holds most important. Like Dr. Maya Angelou once said, "Now that we know better, we can do better." This assessment gives you a powerful tool to know better and then respond accordingly. I'm putting this at the beginning of this book because it sets the tone for movement and momentum going forward.

Choosing to Be a Principled Leader

At the top of this chapter I mentioned in my youth I was lacking knowledge and action on basic principles and universal facts, and I'd like to explain this statement. What exactly are these principles and why are they important? And how do they connect to motivation? General opinions regarding principles can be as varied as there are people in this world; the path you follow greatly depends on who you are and what you value. Yet as true as gravity works in any place on earth, likewise are the solid, foundational principles that work everywhere you go. In my experience as a businessman, a pastor, and a human being, I've noticed the same principles surface as pillars of great leadership.

Leadership is the ability to influence someone to say or do something, and it is a skill that we all have the capacity to learn. We all have the potential to be innovative thinkers, decision makers, solution finders, problem solvers, and agents of change. The lightning is within us. We are the precious container that holds the talent and possibilities for a better, more productive, and joyful tomorrow.

When we ask "What do people need here? What are their problems? What are their pain points?" we are demonstrating principled leadership. We are thinking outside our own needs and considering the needs of others around us—those on our teams, in our organizations, even in our own families. When you let principles like integrity and empathy guide your decision making, you can help others answer these questions and solve their problems. Empowering others and helping them be successful is energizing and inspiring. One of the turning points for me was shifting my attention from myself to other people. Once I began to ask what people's needs are, that was it for me.

Adhering to universal principles is the foundation of strong leadership. By living your principles, you model the very behavior and action that you wish to see in others on your team, and help others solve their problems or answer their questions. You can become a leader anywhere world. The average person is programmed to run away from problems. Leaders run toward the problems. I am grateful that I applied this principle because it helped me build a strong ethical foundation, which in turn helped me see positive growth and results. I was fortunate to stay in my home country of Nigeria because I founded a wonderful school that helped many people establish themselves, learn how to make a living, and become smarter and more confident people.

How are you channeling your principles to guide your ability to lead? Following are the top principles I believe make the best leaders.

Integrity

Integrity is the foundation for enduring success. It is knowing yourself, what you believe, what you stand for, and what you will and will not tolerate. Without integrity, you cannot build trusting relationships.

Integrity is a required behavior of leaders today and is considered one of the highest forms of human intelligence. We don't operate in a vacuum; nobody succeeds alone. Integrity is a quality I most value in leaders. Life's circumstances will always be changing, but your stand on living with integrity should not.

Gone are the days of "Do as I say, not as I do." Truthful leaders do not break the standards they enforce on others. That won't fly in our ever-connected online world. You could find yourself on the wrong end of a TikTok viral video if you are not walking your talk, jeopardizing any success you may have seen to date. Leaders who espouse integrity and honesty are willing to be vulnerable, and therefore show their humanity and admit their mistakes—a relatable quality that sets them apart from elitist cults of personality. When leaders have integrity, what you see is what you get.

The reason I feel so strongly about integrity being the first and most important universal principle is that in the environment in which I grew up, kings, leaders, and figures of authority could not be wrong. Even if they were wrong, they were right! This particular brand of domineering leadership still rears its ugly head around the world. It depends on its powerful positional authority or coercion to secure cooperation. It is ineffective and the world has seen its disastrous results far too many times. A leader's integrity can be built or demolished on their patterns of behavior, and without it, leaders put on a false mask of perfection and pretend to have no flaws. As followers become leaders, they too pretend and become hypocrites; the negative cycle continues.

Personal integrity helps you live authentically and genuinely, and helps build and maintain trust. Once trust is broken, it is very difficult to regain.

Authenticity

Along with integrity, authenticity tells the world you're the genuine article. It is the essence of who you are, not just what you do. Authentic leaders are respected for acting in accordance with their true nature and character—honest, trustworthy, self-assured, and respectful of others, among other attributes. They live their truth. They do not perform in a manner contrary to their self-image.

What sets authentic leaders apart from the pack is their ability to develop self-knowledge. They acknowledge their emotions and intuition, show humanity by being vulnerable and admit mistakes, and never ask another to do what they would not do themselves. William Penn said it best: "No man is fit to command another who cannot command himself." If we are self-aware, we use our mistakes as opportunities to learn, and to teach others. Authentic leaders are responsible for themselves, own their behavior, and refuse to be victim to their own emotions.

Empathy

Among the many basic principles and universal facts leaders should embody is empathy. Empathy is the bridge to understanding the feelings of others and their needs, and I believe it is an important characteristic for a leader to have. I recently read an article in *Forbes* magazine that discussed studies on empathetic leadership, which found such leadership can contribute to positive experiences for people. In fact, 86 percent of people surveyed indicated they better managed their work-life balance when they had leaders who were empathetic.[1]

---

1 Tracy Brower, "Empathy Is the Most Important Leadership Skill According to Research," *Forbes*, September 9, 2021, https://www.forbes.com/sites/tracybrower/2021/09/19/empathy-is-the-most-important-leadership-skill-according-to-research/?sh=4693c1633dc5.

As we move into leadership positions, we sometimes lose the ability to connect with others for reasons of ego, power, or status. How we attend to nurturing the professional and personal relationships in our lives depends on how sensitive we are to being empathetic.

Character

Character describes someone's most noticeable attributes; it's the big picture of our features and traits that form our nature. Someone with good character is worthy of our admiration and trust; they are willing to consistently do the right thing because they are guided by their principles regardless of the consequences. They back up their moral convictions with ethical action. Conversely, someone with bad character is seen as untrustworthy or shady; they choose what is easy over what is just. The difference between the two is obvious.

Ultimately we never rise beyond the capacity of our character because our character is an outward reflection of our true inner workings. The old adage "hire for character, train for skills" still rings true today.

Courage

Principled leadership requires the courage to make bold decisions, take risks, and act on our decisions. Successful leaders know that making decisions requires risk. What if you make the wrong decision and you fail? Instead, you should be asking yourself what will happen if I don't act? What then? Fear can prompt inaction. Remember that indecision is also a decision to take no action at all.

I found courage under what American four-star general Colin Powell wrote in his Leadership Primer:

> Being responsible sometimes means pissing people off. Good leadership involves responsibility to the welfare of the group, which means that some people will get angry at your actions and decisions. It's inevitable, if you're honorable. Trying to get everyone to like you is a sign of mediocrity; you'll avoid the tough decisions, you'll avoid confronting the people who need to be confronted, and you'll avoid offering differential rewards based on differential performance because some people might get upset. Ironically, by procrastinating on the difficult choices, by trying not to get anyone mad, and by treating everyone equally "nicely" regardless of their contributions, you'll simply ensure that the only people you'll wind up angering are the most creative and productive people in your organization.[2]

Of course we all want to be admired and respected by our teams, but in order to be those things, we must have courage first to make the hard decisions and act on those decisions. We must lead with courage. If we make the wrong decisions, we practice humility by admitting doing so and then acting to correct our mistakes. And by practicing such principled leadership, we do not let fear stop us from making bold decisions

What Kind of Leader Do You Want to Be?

Yesterday's Leadership Qualities

- There were bosses and subordinates.
- Bottomline results came before people.
- People asked, "Why me?"
- Setting more policy was the name of the game.

2 Colin Powell, Leadership Primer, PowerPoint presentation, 2006, https://www.hsdl.org/?view&did=467329.

- Leaders liked control and power.
- Leaders were myopic and took a short-range view of things.
- Leaders made rules and focused on how not to break any of them.
- It was all about avoiding change.
- Follow the leader was in vogue and following trends no matter how inefficient the outcome.
- Bosses were right. Subordinates were wrong, even if they were right.

Tomorrow's Leadership Qualities

- There are leaders, potential leaders, and entrepreneurs working together toward a common goal.
- The organization's greatest assets are its people: Human Capital but also its AI.
- Leaders ask smart questions.
- Leaders originate new ideas and encourage doing the right thing and using common sense.
- Leaders empower others and inspire trust and hope at all costs.
- Leaders/entrepreneurs take a long-range view of the possibilities, while envisioning the future and sharing that vision with others.
- Leaders are flexible, innovative and imaginative. They care about people and therefore encourage greater performance and productivity.
- Leaders create and manage change deliberately.
- Leaders are original in their approach. They use and practice real-world techniques and tools.
- Leaders admit when they are wrong to help others learn from their mistakes.

Morale

It is difficult to maintain motivation if you do not place importance on high morale. Both motivation and morale grow from the same seeds—intrinsic beliefs and behaviors. As a leader you want to ensure your organization has high morale. Morale is the enthusiasm, loyalty, and discipline of a person or group regarding a task or job, and it goes beyond the atmosphere in which we work. It's a state of mind and a state of experiencing confidence or enthusiasm within ourselves.

Good morale and attitude is a daily choice. When you choose positivity and optimism, you are making a decision that has the potential to energize your team. When you take on a positive attitude, that becomes your best decision at that moment in time. Choosing a positive and energized attitude will determine your altitude—or how high up you will go in life. High morale lifts you to a higher plane and engages you in greater purpose. It manifests thrill, engagement, and excitement; strong leaders encourage the same in their teams and organizations. Morale is a double-edged sword: when it's good, it taps into your team's enthusiasm and energy; when it's low, it smolders creativity and is harmful to your spirits. Principled leaders are committed to building high morale teams. They set the tone for the behavior they wish to see.

Tips on Building a High Morale Atmosphere

- **Lead by example.** By modeling the behavior you wish to see, you set the tone for the morale of your organization.
- **Be trustworthy.** You can establish trust and engagement by demonstrating consistent behavior and intentions.
- **Communicate.** Establish good communication and clear expectations.

- **Be genuine,** authentic, and humble.
- **Radiate a positive attitude.** It is a powerful magnet that attracts motivated and energetic people to dive in.
- **Stay creative.** Creative energy makes the difference between getting the job done and getting it done with distinction and enthusiasm.

CHAPTER 2:

Core Values and Agile Change Guide Behaviors and Build Confidence

Just as your GPS plots your course as you travel, your core values serve as a guide for your thoughts and behavior. A solid foundation of values and morals helps steer you through every situation you find yourself in, be it at work, at home, in your community, wherever. Values such as integrity, honesty, self-respect, dependability, self-discipline, and countless others should guide your decisions. They give you peace of mind that you are doing right by the situation, that you are making the best possible decision given your choices at the time. As a leader you are going to face situations where your values may conflict, for example such as when you face a conundrum on whether to meet an important deadline (responsibility value) or to help a colleague during a crisis (community service value). The values you commit to and act upon, as well as your ability to accept and embrace change, consistently reveal to others your true character—not the other way around.

Identifying and living by your core values is at the heart of true and genuine personal authenticity. In all of my books I have tried to convey the importance of this lesson. Knowing which value to apply to each individual situation is a marker of growth as a professional and as a mature adult, as well as a showing of your true character to act and make a decision in any situation, crisis or not. You will not always get it right, but by using your values to guide your decisions and welcome agile change, you are making a choice to move forward. Making decisions means taking a risk; the bigger the choice, the bigger the risk. Making no choice is actually a choice, too—and that is not what a successful leader does. Using your core values to guide your decisions means you are actively trying to do the right thing with every decision you make.

Both people and organizations have values, and both are as varied as the people and the organizations themselves. Take for example, GE. Today their corporate values of Act with Humility, Lead with Transparency, and Deliver with Focus, are a reflection of an organization that had to shift and pivot its corporate values after leadership failures nearly destroyed the century-old company. I am oversimplifying, of course, but my main point is an organization's values must shift over time to reflect the changing external climate, culture, and environment. GE did not abandon all its values; it shifted its values and put its energies, resources, and actions toward what was going to keep the company successful and moving in the right direction. An organization that has its values chiseled into stone becomes stagnant and outdated. It does not grow. The same can be said for people. Our core values should guide us but we must remain vigilant and aware of the shifting patterns around us, and apply our values accordingly. This, too, is the essence of agile change.

Building an Enviable Culture with Core Values

Core values are the foundation upon which great organizational cultures are built. Yet it can be elusive how to create a strong company culture in which everyone from a frontline supervisor to boardroom members feels empowered to act on their values. Successful leaders create winning and encouraging environments where everyone thrives. Values-based organizations attract top talent and top-rated performers, from customer and employee satisfaction to a solid return on investment and profitability. Stories, like I've included here in this book from my own work and life experiences, help a culture build rituals, traditions, and legacies. These become the legs of the stool that hold everyone up with pride and greater personal satisfaction.

Here are my four tips on how to help create a world-class culture through core values. Be sure to put your own unique spin on things because that's what will make your leadership development shine:

1. **Be the example.** Demonstrate that doing the right thing is the right thing to do. Be the man or the woman in the mirror. Before taking action, ask yourself: Does this action make sense in light of the values we've created and abide by in our organization? If the answer is yes, then you have a green light to move ahead and try something new.
2. **You can only influence behavior.** You can't force it or make it happen. Positive culture is an organic result of high morale and good behavior. How do you encourage and empower others to flourish and thrive no matter what the circumstances?
3. **Take care of the inside and the outside will take care of itself.** What your company exhibits to the public is a reflection of what is going on behind the scenes. How you treat your valued customers can never be the opposite of how you treat each other within the walls

of your company. No one can be made to smile and feel valued. How do you treat your people? How do they treat each other? Similarly with your own family, when you take care of what is happening under your own roof first, the chances of your family members behaving the same way when they walk out the front door is highly likely. It works the same in any organization. Provide for your employees and their light will shine on your customers.

4. **Take conscious action.** The culture you desire can be created on shared strategic values and financial responsibility. What blueprint will you create to be the best in your field? Write it down. Then put the blueprint into action consciously and with heart.

When you base your decisions and act accordingly on your core values, you are aligning your actions with your beliefs, your values. We often model our morals and core values based on what we have grown up with or what we have become accustomed to. Many of us learned our values system from our families, our communities, our faith. We also adopt value traits of those whom we admire and respect. When you are guided by your internal values system, you tend to know your "why"—the reason you do what you do. For many, their "why" is their family or their faith. Your "why" should be guided by and based on your core values. Because, like the saying goes, if you do not stand for something, you will fall for anything. Your "why" matters because it is your past, present, and future. The decisions you make and the actions you take are the habits you form over a lifetime; they should reflect your core values because you cannot build a good life and make smart decisions based on a faulty values foundation.

> **"CORE VALUES HELP US TO CREATE A STRONGER FRAMEWORK THAT ALLOWS US TO EVALUATE AND MAKE BETTER CHOICES AS LEADERS."**
> —Dr. Sam Adeyemi

Drop the Plastic Ball

Life is a constant juggle of conflicting priorities. A wise man named Brian Dyson, the former CEO of Coca-Cola, explained that the priorities we juggle are like juggling balls of glass and plastic. The glass balls are the priorities, such as family, work, health, friends, and faith; they are the important ones. When you drop one, the damage could range from a small scratch to a total loss. The risk is greater and the stakes are higher. You must prioritize catching the glass balls. Some of the balls, however, are made of plastic. The plastic balls are smaller balls within the same priorities as above; only they are resilient and they bounce. The risk is lesser and if you drop one, the consequences may not be as dire. And you can pick them up and put them back into the juggle.

You will have times in your life when you are going to drop a ball. You are human; it is going to happen. Just make sure that when you drop a ball, you drop the plastic one.

Agile Change and Core Values Transform Culture

Long gone are the days of top-down change management. Instead, it is about agile change within leadership. Change must be fluid and flexible to be influential and to help people grow and move forward. Picture an inverted pyramid. This is where the pyramid is upside down. The CEO and Board of Directors are at the bottom point of the pyramid. At the wider, flatter top are the customers and frontline employees who drive processes and current trends. Organization charts of the past no longer work in an agile society. Agile leaders soften the blow of necessary change. They make change desirable, innovative, fun, and greatly anticipated. Agile change is evidence-based and not a trend. Agile change helps us all to be better leaders who exercise strong core values that lead to enviable cultures.

A Close Up Perspective

As the CEO for a global leadership and consultancy organization, I realize the tremendous impact that our core values and agile change can have in an organization. They often provide a lighthouse that guides people's actions and decision making that can shape the course of future outcomes. I believe leaders, just like you and the aspiring leaders on your team, can play a significant role in leveraging influence at every level. Here are several ways you can be more intentional about your efforts in this area.

Create a blueprint and define your personal values. Even if you cannot list your personal values off the top of your head, you live by them daily. Whether we realize it or not, we often prioritize things repeatedly—like family over money, hard work over laziness, serving others over self-gratification. When I ask someone what is your main priority, I can tell you that their core values will dictate the true answer. For example, if I ask a man or woman, "What is your priority?" And he or she replies it is family, the next thing I do is to look at how this person spends his or her time and his money. If they're gone from home traveling 300 days of the year and spending most of their money on new clothes or social activities, I know the priority stated is truly not family, unless the family is included in all of these activities. How we spend our time, how we behave and how we choose to responsibly use our financial resources are strong indicators of our core values and will almost always be the true test of our most meaningful priorities.

Be sure your values align with the values you set for your organization. By doing this, you will be able to commit wholeheartedly to the achievement of the organization's goals and this will thereby enhance everyone's productivity and performance, not to mention their happiness on the job.

When your personal goals align with the values of your company, you and others will fit into the organization's culture more easily, thereby cultivating strong working relationships. Misalignment between personal values and the organization creates conflict, miscommunication, and sometimes resentment among other team members and can cause deep dissatisfaction. If the organization's values are irreconcilable with yours, it may be in your best interest and the interest of your team to plan your exit. No one will benefit under these contradictory conditions. So analyze this carefully. Give it the attention and respect it deserves.

Create and build a list of core values. Make this your cultural blueprint for moving forward and achieving success. When you do this you will be creating a winning environment where everyone thrives. Explain to your teams that creating a list of core values gives the company a North Star to fix their sights on. This is an important point. Further explain that by clearly defining what your organization stands for and values, you give others a navigational compass for making good decisions, improving behavior and maturity, and growing forward and appreciating success—not taking anything for granted.

Continue to model your organization's values. In their bestselling book *The Leadership Challenge: How to Make Extraordinary Things Happen in Organizations,* James Pouzes and Barry Posner discuss how to Model the Way. There is great dissonance in leadership when the actions of leaders contradict the stated values of the organization. People get the message loud and clear: "The stated values are for window dressing. It's okay to do what you like." So always set the tone. For example, leaders of an organization should not expect teams to sacrifice spending if they, too, are not willing to make any sacrifices themselves. When you model the values you set, it is easier to achieve respect, consistency, and support from your team, and most likely happier employees. Hypocrisy creates resentment and when resentment enters the front door, love, appreciation, and commitment will leave out the back door.

Let core values attract top talent to your organization. Strive to make your culture and values as famous as your brand. When you align people with values, you're also building a strong relevant brand. You'll be building a compelling framework and implementing a people strategy that will last for years to come. Alignment is a wakeup call for today's hiring. You go beyond recruiting and begin creating a sustainable talent system. Hiring those that do not align with your blueprint of values can do irreparable damage because people then contradict what's most important. A leader cannot perform in a manner that is inconsistent with what he or she claims is most important. Therefore, the hiring process should include not just competence but character. I discuss branding to attract top talent in chapter 7 of this book. Cross-reference my points for a clearer picture.

Reward behavior and privately correct and redirect misbehavior. Human behaviorists write about evidence-based positive reward. Great leaders understand that catching someone doing something right (not wrong), then rewarding the behavior is a great way to build employee morale. Some organizations go as far as to actually celebrate people's mistakes. This means that they acknowledge the error made (in a positive way, not correcting or dressing down publicly) and share it with others in team meetings so that they too will not repeat the same mistake. Doing this can save thousands, sometimes hundreds of thousands of dollars in possible future errors. People are human; always offer a person the benefit of the doubt and help people to save face and not feel embarrassed. When someone is given the opportunity to correct and redirect they usually do. But unfortunately sometimes a person's departure from the organization is the most reasonable ending. I can't think of a leader who enjoys firing an employee or terminating a relationship. This is among our least favorite duties so you want to give a person the chance to correct and redirect his or her actions. Yet sometimes it is best for someone to move on. And if there is disappointment or failure that is beyond repair, you must think of the other players involved. One person can deeply affect the entire team negatively or even drive good workers away. Remember, people leave people, not organizations. Everyone should not have to suffer for one person's poor behavior. Keep in mind there are positive outcomes from many termination situations. Often great self-awareness for both the leader and the worker are the result of parting ways. The goal is to terminate with mutual benefit and leave smiling and satisfied. Isn't that the primary goal of every customer-driven organization and leader?

Remember, core values and acceptance of an ever-changing environment will always drive leadership success. Values first is the name of the game because it creates an environment where hard decisions are made easier, positive cultures are defined and redefined, and the capacity to fulfill future vision and goals become stronger than ever before. Lead from your heart and you will never be misled or mislead others.

> **"RESPECTING OUR VALUES WILL MAKE UP OUR SOUL PRINT OF LEADERSHIP STANDARDS."**
>
> —Dr. Sam Adeyemi

In this chapter we have acknowledged the importance of a leader establishing and abiding by core values. Core values are the essence of future leadership. Also, when we practice agile change, we invite flexible thinking into the organization. We welcome everyone's differences and respect that every person evolves differently and at a different pace.

■■■

How did this chapter shift your mindset regarding the importance of core values in leadership? List your core values as a leader here. How will you help others on the team channel their core values into their working environment? How might this transition into your personal development, as well? Explain ways you will implement agile change going forward.

____

____

____

____

____

What do you see as the possibilities of using these tools as a leader?

____

____

____

____

____

How do you envision becoming and implementing these leadership possibilities? How do your core values shape you as a leader? How will agility regarding change and transformation serve you best?

____

____

____

____

____

Next, let's calibrate our compass as leaders. You'll be writing your own story. But first, I'll share a few of mine to help pave the way.

CHAPTER 3:

Life Lessons and Stories from Dr. Sam: A Personal Roadmap

Dear Leader, why am I sharing my personal stories with you? Because storytelling is one of the most powerful ways we can train and lead others to success. When people hear a real-life example from one of their own leaders, they remember those stories and try to relate to them personally. Often this becomes a personal roadmap for the up-and-coming leader. It establishes a feeling of confidence. It says, "If you can do it, I can do it, too."

Sharing our life's lessons inspires, lifts, and grows the next generation of leaders. And they are not just stories of success. Often great leaders share their stories of failure or despair and those lead to lessons learned and new ways to approach problems and challenges. I particularly like this quote by Winston Churchill, and believe it sums up my feelings on this matter succinctly: "Success is not final. Failure is not fatal. It is the courage to continue that counts."

> "SUCCESS IS NOT FINAL. FAILURE IS NOT FATAL. IT IS THE COURAGE TO CONTINUE THAT COUNTS."
>
> —Winston Churchill

In this chapter, I am sharing just a few of my personal stories. What story or stories will you share with other aspiring leaders along the way? At the end of this chapter, I have provided a place for you to write your own story.

Meet People Where They Are—Give Them What They Need

Many years ago, as a pastor in my hometown in Nigeria, I began addressing poverty—which was a huge challenge in my area—in my Sunday messages. The Bible has many stories about entrepreneurship so that's where I began. People wanted to hear these messages and they packed the church. The managing editor for the then-leading financial newspaper in Nigeria got wind of what I was doing and extended an opportunity for me to write a column in his paper. Over a short period, the newspaper's sales increased greatly. The managing editor told me it was because the average person who never would have bought a financial paper was now buying his financial newspaper because of my column. And here's why: just like with my Sunday messages, I wrote my column so people could understand my leadership lessons clearly. Leaders must remember to speak directly to people around them, simply, directly, and kindly. Albert Einstein wrote a good deal about the importance of simple messaging so that everyone can feel included and understand even the most complex communication. At university, standing among other mathematicians and professors, Einstein often became perturbed with his colleagues when they would speak over the heads of others with words and terminology only a fellow professor or scientist might understand.

So first, you've got to identify and find the platforms people are using, and reach them where they are and at the level where they will comprehend your meaning. That's where you can best say what you have to say and where people will hear you. When you meet people where they are and give them what they need, they will listen to what you're saying. Remember, it's about the other person. It's not about you feeling smarter, wanting to impress others, or feeding your ego.

The other critical component of all this is learning how to truly become a good communicator. From my perspective, the best communicators are outstanding listeners. They don't wait for their turn to talk next. They are fully engaged and in a receiving mode. Once they fully listen to the information being presented, they are able to ask smarter questions. When a leader asks quality questions, others feel valued and receptive to constructive guidance and corrective feedback. It's this action that meets the other person right where they are and then provides solutions to their pain points. I have always tried to practice this skillset as a leader and it has served me and others well. My humble beginnings in Africa were most likely my most valuable classroom.

Perception Is Often Reality: Take Control of Your Personal Branding

Five days after my 28th birthday, I was hosting a radio show on teaching people how to succeed. My first broadcast was about the power of persistence. It had taken me many years and many struggles to land this radio program, so the irony of persistence being the subject of my first broadcast is not lost on me.

I was young and had a lot of self-doubt. I thought I needed to be successful before I was qualified to talk to people about success. I thought I needed certain achievements to be there, like a beautiful office, a lot of money, a nice car. I took a chance and spoke anyway because I knew my messages were valuable for people to hear. And I'm so grateful that I kept going despite my fears about whether I was qualified to speak or not because what was about to happen was truly amazing and altered the trajectory of my career—actually, my entire life.

People began to tune in. I had a real audience. My credibility was enhanced. My radio show was on the air just once a week, and people would be scrambling into their offices to find a radio so they could listen to it. Today I appear on popular podcasts and a variety of internet radio programs or on my own YouTube channel. However, at that time when I was starting out, it occurred to me that being on the radio resolved some of my questions about establishing my own branding.

For a time before I began my show, I wondered why people weren't inviting me to speak at their conferences. I loved to speak and thought I had good messages to share. The moment I started the broadcast, invitations to speak began rolling in. Then it hit me. People did not know me and they did not know my message. They did not know my unique value or what set me apart from other radio personalities. Now that I was on the radio, the audience got to know me and know my message. So if a conference had to do with success or leadership, then it was likely my name would come up.

I'm often asked if success is what is sometimes termed "a numbers game"—well, yes and no. The more exposure you have, the more impressions you make, and the more likely it is you will be recognized as a subject matter expert and invited to a place at the table. In advertising, the term *repeated* or *frequent impressions* is meaningful. Few people buy a product or service the first time they see or hear about it. It typically takes a minimum of three to seven impressions before the consumer actually listens up or tries out the brand.

We see the same repetitiveness in social media as influencers work hard to gain followers and likes. It's the same when a keynote speaker is chosen for a conference, or a facilitator is asked to participate in a worldwide training event, or a candidate is selected for a job promotion or a new hire is sought out. There are many brilliant speakers and trainers to choose from, and many wonderful candidates for high-level positions, but it is the most familiar, relevant, highly exposed individuals who are typically invited to submit a proposal or actually take the stage at an event, get invited to an interview, or offered a promotion within the organization. Visibility is key.

Today in social media we see the enormous power of social media influencers. As I mentioned earlier, what makes them influential is their repeated messaging. That is when followers rise from hundreds to thousands to millions. So the concept has never really changed, just the delivery of the messaging. At some point the consumer must reach out and select the person, product, or service of their choosing. Competition can be fierce. Therefore, strong messaging and personal and professional branding is critical. I seemed to intuitively understand this at a young age and that is why I want to share these insights with you here in my book. Listen to your gut. Follow your intuition and greater purpose and passion for what you do.

My advice to young entrepreneurs is to find opportunities to serve and to add value. Figure out what you are good at doing, what is normal for you, what you excel at—but that which others do not have. Stand out. But not from an ego perspective, but from a value-added quality and perspective. You've got to identify that unique value. Look for ways to serve. When I was on the radio, what I was saying was second nature and normal to me, but it was not normal to the people who were hearing me. The radio gave me a platform from where I could serve others. Branding positions you in the eyes of others and shapes other people's perceptions of you. You may have heard the term "Perception is reality." Well, it often can be. Living up to the perception and delivering what you promise is what is most important. That's what will make you a leader of integrity. Even though I was quite young at the time, my listeners thought I was older because of my messaging on success and entrepreneurship. Always allow your core values to shine through your branding, as if to say, "Hey! I'm the genuine article!" "I'm the real deal." "I am one of the best in my business and I am here to help lead the way." Mutual trust and respect will always be at the forefront of every relationship.

Integrity Is Currency—It's Like Cash In the Bank

Dr. David Oyedepo made a statement many years ago that rings in my mind: if you don't have values, you don't have value. This struck me as a very powerful message. When you have strong values and you live by those values, you resist the temptations of making a quick buck in a crooked way, which may gain you something of material value in the short-term, but in the long term, you will be losing your integrity and self-respect. In addition, mutual trust is at stake.

I tell people that integrity is cash, it is your currency, if you really understand how it works. For example, if I needed some amount of money right now, there are people I can reach out to who they wouldn't think twice before giving me the money. Why? Because I have never deceived or misled them before—I let my values lead me. So you must communicate your values clearly and live by your values, because you will be respected for living authentically through your values. When you have values, you have leadership currency and that is like cash in the bank.

People don't have to agree with your values. They don't have to agree with your decisions. Leaders must make tough calls and initiate difficult conversations. Others will respect you for having boundaries, for being able to say yes or no. You are mistaken if you think people are going to like you because you say yes to everything they suggest because they will not respect you. Being a "yes person" is not a marker for success.

In the organizations that I lead, I try hard to model the values I wish to see in others. Nothing erodes the credibility of a leader like hypocrisy. In one of my organizations, for example, accountability is one of the core values. And because I built this organization in Africa—an environment where a founder or leader typically wields a lot of power—people find it surprising that I have made myself accountable to the Board of Directors.

At the management level, my team and I make the decisions, prepare the budget, and set the objectives for the year. We show our integrity and our transparency. Then I take everything to the Board of Directors, and whatever they decide, I abide by it. I have found that it gives people that serve with me a sense of safety, and it buys me a lot of respect. It also provides the critical ingredient of empowerment. And empowering others translates into cash.

A famous story about empowerment is how the well-known five-star hotel chain The Ritz Carlton would allow employees at every level to spend up to $2,000 per hotel guest to solve a problem and not have to reach out to a manager or higher authority for approval. (Note that

The Ritz Carlton is now part of mega hotel giant Marriott Bonvoy and new policies may be in place in certain locations because of different property management groups. But the point remains the same—everyone's empowered and accountable.) My specific point is that by making myself accountable to a Board of Directors, I was empowering the Board and our shareholders and stakeholders to do what was best for the business. The trust and reputation I have as a result is immeasurable. The payoff, like currency to be spent, is ongoing. As a result, our employee retention is quite high. Even when conditions are not perfect, as we experienced during the COVID pandemic, we still found that our people remained committed because the respect is there. People feel valued and empowered. This remains our greatest currency to this day.

When People Feel Valued They Become Shareholders and Intrinsically Motivated

A shareholder is always a stakeholder, but a stakeholder is not always a shareholder. What I mean by this is that shareholders own a little piece of the action and are committed to its success. When we own something, we usually take better care of it, be it our business, our material possessions, our relationships. It lends you a greater sense of responsibility for the outcome. When you're a shareholder, you own your part in every interaction you encounter—your behavior, your messaging, your thoughts. A good example is when you rent a car. When you return the car do you get it washed and detailed? Do you change the oil and have the tires rotated? No. Because it is not your car. You return it at the end of your rental period and the company does all of those things—because it's their car, not yours. You may have a stake in the rental process but you don't own the vehicle.

I think things begin to fall apart when leaders in an organization do not show their integrity or core values. They do not act as owners who value what they have—and what they have is human capital, made up of actual humans who have feelings and a need to be respected, appreciated, and recognized. Successful leaders own their behavior and its consequences.

There has never been a better time to understand this concept than today. Many workers are not feeling integrity from their leaders or from the organization where they work. They do not feel respected or appreciated. In fact, today's younger generation has experienced more disruptions than previous generations have so they tend to be more flexible and strategic in their thinking and more mobile in their job pursuits. They speak with their feet by stepping away when they quit an undesirable working environment. And please remember, people leave people, not jobs or companies, marriages, or organizations. They walk away from people. It is therefore very important for leaders to demonstrate strong values like integrity and empathy, and dare I say love as well (when we celebrate the value of our fellow humans). In many companies now, human capital is a line item on the balance sheet, not just equipment and office furniture. Many organizations have replaced the term *Human Resources* with *People Department.* The first to do this was Southwest Airlines when it was led by its president and CEO, the late Herb Kelleher, but the airlines continues to use *People* (and they capitalize it in all documents) to convey this strong message. And speaking of love, the airline's trading symbol on the New York Stock exchange is LUV.

When the core values of the workers and the leaders and organization are misaligned, that will eventually show on your bottom line in costs of decreased employee retention and increased onboarding when dissatisfied people leave for greener pastures. Humans are the greatest assets on this planet. Aim to be a shareholder who values and loves people for more than their ability to produce. When you do, you will create intrinsic motivation. That is motivation that comes from within, not just a salary or an incentive. Intrinsic motivation is powerful.

Here's a simple example of what it looks like. An employee who is walking across the parking lot to their car sees a candy wrapper on the ground. A motivated employee may just keep walking knowing that it will be picked up by grounds people tomorrow. But a worker who is intrinsically motivated will stop and pick up the small piece of trash and discard it because he or she feels ownership in the business and a special kind of pride in their work that can only come from intrinsic motivation and the feeling of a job well done. When you value and respect your people, you commit to being a shareholder with a stake in not only your future but in the future of others.

Practice Extreme Ownership

My job is to make sure my people become successful as strategic leaders. I earned my doctorate in strategic leadership and it remains my passion. I believe in the capacity and potential of every person on my team, and I believe each of my team members can actually do what I'm doing. Of course, I want them to know their job, but I also expect them to look out for the organization as a whole, and to step in when they see something that's not right. I genuinely empower them to act on behalf of this organization.

Empowerment is a great thing unless it's used carelessly. When it's thrown around casually with no values to back it up, it doesn't exist.

That's when leaders teeter on the edge of hypocrisy— sending message of empowerment with strings—empowering others to action but only if they act according to how they want others to act. That becomes a failure if there's punishment or retribution for someone who takes action or makes a mistake. People will make mistakes; they should not be punished for it. Empowerment is one of the greatest gifts you can give an employee. I describe this in detail and with an example in my Integrity is Currency story, above. When a person is not allowed to take accountability, learn from their mistakes, or otherwise feels humiliation because they must have approval for every little thing, you have lost the title of being a true leader and sadly you may extinguish the light of your aspiring leaders. This book is a testament to the commitment my team and I have to help you to become the best leader possible. I feel strongly this book is one of the most important empowerment tools you may use in your entire career. And we are here to support you on your journey.

When you practice extreme ownership, you are responsible— for not only the successes but also the failures. I have a wonderful example of exactly this to share. I asked my team to please pay attention to the places where we interact with the public—social media, video meetings, presentations. I asked them all to own it. I wanted everyone to take responsibility for how we appear to our audience because it's the little things—a misspelling or wrong grammar here, a misplaced graphic there—that chip away at our branding and how others perceive our organization. My team assured me that they were up to it.

One afternoon, we hosted a video conference that my team coordinated. I was not leading this session so I attended using my phone, which did not show my full name. The person leading the session was not aware the wrong chart was showing. Before I could text some members of the team to correct the issue, somebody stepped in and fixed the mistake—live on the video chat.

I thought, "Fantastic! This is what I have been saying!" Even though it was not his job to do so, a team member took responsibility because we're a team and we're interacting with the public. I sent him a text message to say thank you, that was fantastic that you took care of it. He did not know I was attending the session and was very surprised that I witnessed his fantastic act of extreme ownership. When everyone takes responsibility for the success of the team, everyone succeeds.

Create a Culture Council of Fresh Ideas Through Fresh Eyes

Leaders set the expectations of the behavior for the team and must lead by example, including with how they communicate. How team members communicate with one another and how they receive the ideas and inspirations of one another all depends on how the leader fosters lines of communication.

On my team, most of us are introverts, but the downside of that is most of the conversations we have are inside our own heads! I as the leader set the ground rules that all communications and all ideas are welcome—no matter who you are, no matter what level you are in the organization, everybody's creativity has value because that is one of the values of our organization. We accept ideas, appreciate the people, and value what they bring to the table.

Just imagine the potential of what we could accomplish if all our ideas were out of our heads and onto the table! I encouraged my team to say something when they see something that needs to be implemented, instead of keeping it inside their head. The best way to encourage open communications is to set the ground rules to establish a safe environment where all ideas from all people are welcome.

There's a saying that if you want to improve the processes and services of your organization, ask the people who are actually performing that job daily. If you want to improve janitorial services in your office, then have the janitors submit their recommendations. They are the ones doing the job and know best, not the vice president of a division. If you want to know how to improve delivery services in your area, ask the truck drivers and the shipping department for their ideas, not the regional manager. Makes sense doesn't it? Yet we fail to recognize everyone who can bring their brilliant ideas to the table and therefore we miss out on some of the best ideas that may ensure our success and greater customer care and satisfaction.

Now, in Africa young people generally do not correct their elders, and the average African understands this. It is likely if you are a young person who is vocal, you will be corrected and shown your place. Also in organizations, sometimes leaders perceive their ego is being challenged when junior colleagues contradict their ideas, whereas junior colleagues are just trying to express themselves. The senior colleagues tend to look at them and shut them down. It is not only in Africa that this happens, but that's been my journey and my experience.

So my wife and I did something revolutionary in one of our organizations. When we bring in new members into the management team, we established a culture of talking to them with just the two of us after they are hired because they are coming in with fresh eyes.

We tell them that it is very important for them to express themselves in those first six months, to let us know whatever they think needs improvement or whatever could be done differently. We tell them that some of us have been here since the inception of the organization more than 20 years ago so there are those among us that do not see with new eyes. We tell them that as a newcomer, they're likely to see certain things. The fresh perspective is appreciated on both sides. Some companies offer what is called a Culture Council to onboard new ideas and new employees in a fun and creative way.

Head, Heart, Hands, Feet

When we have power we should use it to harness the power of human life and its greatest potential. When you have power but have no love, the likelihood of you overreaching yourself is high. Human nature and power do not make a good combination except when you put love in the mix. So whether it's people within your organization, your friends, colleagues, family, whomever—just learn to love people. Don't sacrifice people to achieve success; rather make sacrifices to help people succeed. You will also succeed.

Think of leadership as you would the human body: head, heart hands, and feet. Here's an example:

- **Head.** A person's head holds all of their intellectual property, IQ, experiences, and wisdom.
- **Heart.** The heart is the heartbeat of the organization. It drives everything. It represents love. It shows us how to love our people, love our community, and love ourselves.

- **Hands.** Our hands represent implementation of all the leadership lessons we learn. We can learn these lessons but if we don't apply them, then what good are they? Our hands allow us to put new ideas into play.
- **Feet.** This is where you stand and put one foot in front of the other. Leadership is not a long-distance marathon. It is a journey that we all take one step at a time. Our feet allow us to stand strong, find our balance, and move forward.

And now as we grow forward, we can integrate the human spirit into the new amazing and futuristic ways artificial intelligence and so many other means will be used for global leadership in medicine, law, engineering, technology, teaching, climate change, environmental stability, political and human rights compassion, and so much more.

And dear leader, it all starts with love.

Now it's your turn. I would like you to write your own leadership story that you are willing to share with others. Start by establishing the point you want to make. Is this a story about overcoming failure? Is it a story about building a business from scratch? Is it a story about making wise choices? Whatever your story is, start by deciding what point it is you are going to make. Then begin writing. Start with an interesting sentence or two that becomes the beginning of your story. Then provide the content or meat of the matter. Finally, explain the relevance and reason you are sharing your story with others. If you approach it this way, writing your story will be easy and a tool you can share with others. The power of our personal stories builds leadership goals, hopes, and dreams above and beyond our imagination. I look forward to reading your stories. Please post them on my social media and how this chapter impacted you as a leader.

My Leadership Story

By ____________________________________(your name here)

____

____

____

____

____

____

____

In this chapter we have acknowledged the importance of our life lessons and how to share them with others. You have written your own story of leadership and hopefully you will share your story with others and coach them how to write his or her own, as well.

■■■

How did this chapter on storytelling and creating life lessons affect you? Did you find it helpful to revisit your life experiences? Was it emotional? Did this chapter help you to recall stories of your past that you can implement as learning lessons today?

____

____

____

____

____

____

____

____

What do you see as the possibilities for storytelling as a leadership tool going forward?

____

____

____

____

____

____

____

____

How will you breathe life into the possibilities of your life lessons and story?

____

____

____

____

____

____

____

____

Coming up—today's multiple generations as leaders. Global leadership has a new face. Or should I say it has many faces and many age groups? Get ready to practice multi-generational leadership methods in the next chapter.

Part Two

CHAPTER 4:

Leadership Success in a Multi-Generational Workplace

Never in the history of the world have there been so many generations working under the same roof together. Frankly, this scenario has caused some frustration within the generational divide and understandably so. Twenty-year old workers on teams with 60+-year old workers can make for enormously different views and perspectives. However, there's a remarkable, positive side to this new way of working and leading that no one can deny.

> **"ACROSS ALL THE GENERATIONS THERE IS AS MUCH FOR EACH OF US TO LEARN AS THERE IS TO TEACH OTHERS."**
> —Dr. Sam Adeyemi

Today's global and multi-generational workplace looks much different than it once did. But I'd argue that in fact it's a stronger, more culturally rich, and more sustainable work environment. And unlike the past, most workers do not stay in one organization for decades recycling stale ideas until their retirement. Workers are incentivized to remain relevant, keep up, and move at breakneck speed in some cases.

Things change rapidly and people move on. In fact, global leaders advise not to expect more than two or three good years and commitment from top talent. Workers evolve. Their passion for life is greater than ever. As a result, there exists a great age diversity in today's working environment. Leaders are now required to instill purpose in aspiring leaders and especially in a multi-generational workplace. Here's one of my secrets you can try.

Whenever you are about to initiate a change or act on a new company goal, you can instill passion and purpose by using this Five Ps Formula. These techniques might help you engage teams of diverse employees in meetings, or start a new project, form a new project management team, or initiate brainstorming sessions.

The Five Ps Formula: Purpose, Processes, Payoffs, Passion, and Pride

Instill Purpose

A savvy leader knows what the ultimate goal is and strives to help others achieve it. He or she understands the time constraints, what actions are needed to be successful, and what it will take to accomplish the goal. Giving the team all the information you can upfront is imperative to everyone's success and will build inner-purpose by instilling trust and empowerment. These are ingredients that leaders worldwide use to take people to the next higher level and bring about great confidence in workers—no matter what age or background.

Initiate Innovative Processes

In order to function as a team and reach goals, proper processes need to be established, just like in this book. We established a process model right at the beginning. Before you even began reading, you could see what the process was going to be and could immediately identify a relatable model you could share with others. That helped move you ahead right away in your leadership skills. When everyone knows the proper steps to take, purpose and pride are instilled in the team. People feel trusted to make confident decisions on the project, and it is an open and safe environment for them to brainstorm and share successes and improvements in the processes along the way. Establishing processes also defines the decision making process. So that's an extra bonus.

Know the Payoffs

Competent leaders help their diverse and multi-generational teams visualize what the payoffs will be when the projects are completed. This gives the team the drive and desire to reach the final goals of the projects. The payoff is when the ultimate goal is reached and the team can reflect on what went well and what could be improved upon in the future. This is a time when your team members can validate each person's input, from older, more seasoned employees to new college grads, and respect that individual for the value he or she brought to the project. Perhaps you had a Traditionalist mentoring a Generation Y employee, or a Baby Boomer mentoring a Generation Xer, Z gen, or Nexter. All generations enjoy reaching a goal and seeing the payoff instills pride and joy in their work.

Pour in the Passion

Leaders can instill passion in their workplace by allowing each team to function as a well-oiled machine—not by micromanaging them. When leaders trust their employees and empower them to be creative and imaginative, they instill a passion that cannot be stopped. If employees are coming to work every day without passion, they will not produce the desired result and can potentially be toxic to the rest of the team. Empower others, make everyone feel like part of the team, and let each person's individual attributes contribute to the organization's success. Organizations that practice this often become benchmark examples for global excellence.

Pride

Underscoring all of these actions is simply pride. When someone takes pride in the organization, in their fellow workers, and in themselves, the possibilities are endless. People need to be intrinsically motivated. Sure, people are motivated by reward for a job well done, but initially the motivation has to come from within.

Do you recall the story I told earlier about my teammate who corrected a graphic during a presentation even though it was not specifically his job to do so but he did it anyway? That's taking pride in your company and where you work and who you work with and for. That's intrinsic. No reward, just good behavior.

What will you do today to add the Five Ps Formula to your meetings, tasks, projects, or day-to-day interactions with your teams? Refer to the sidebar for an exercise that tests how well you are using the Five Ps.

How Effectively Are You Using the Five Ps Formula as a Leadership Tool?

Circle True or False for each statement about your leadership methods to indicate if you are using this process.

Everyone on the team understands what's required, outcomes, and desired results.	True	False
Each team member feels comfortable communicating openly in a safe environment.	True	False
Each person is trusted and empowered to take justified risks to make the best decisions for the team.	True	False
Each member of the team fully participates in the meeting, project, or task.	True	False
Each team member is encouraged to bring their individual perspective without fear of reprisal.	True	False
Each team member understands the proper decision making process.	True	False
Each team member is fully engaged and focused on desired results.	True	False
Each team member exhibits passion in their piece of the project or task.	True	False

If you have:

- 7–8 marked true, you have a fully engaged multi-generational team.
- 5–6 marked true, you may have some engagement issues and need to refocus your team and provide them with additional tools or training and empower them to work toward the goals. Check out our Leadership Certification Program for a deep dive on all of this.
- 1–4 marked true, your team is in jeopardy of failure and unless drastic steps are taken, the project may fail and the goals and objectives will not be met.

Other Tips for Communicating and Minding Generational Gaps

One major issue in managing generational gaps is leader-to-follower relationships. Leaders who are younger sometimes struggle when they are charged with managing their more seasoned employees, especially if they are promoted over them. And older leaders sometimes struggle to manage their younger workers because of technical know-how or the speed at which things move and unfold. One way to bridge this gap is to show that you care by respecting everyone's time, asking for their opinions, treating people with respect, mentoring others, and trusting that they will do the work required with integrity and good intention.

To show others that you care, demonstrate a genuine interest in things that interest them and learn about them as people. For example, ask about what their communication preferences are and what makes them tick. Acknowledge employees for their experience and the value they bring to the organization. Every employee wants to feel valued, respected, and as though they have made an important contribution to the organization. People want to feel they are a part of something bigger than themselves. If you help them feel that way, they will work more cohesively together and, more importantly, be dedicated and invested in the success of the team.

Build a Bridge and Get Over the Generational Divide

Below are leadership techniques and commitments that bring multi-generational workplaces closer.

- Build a workplace culture of trust and sustainable talent.
- Appreciate the unique and valuable differences in others.
- Accept that a "one-size-fits-all" mentality no longer works.
- Find your own voice and your own unique ways to communicate with every generation. The combination of every person will build a culture of diversity and undeniable effectiveness.
- Demonstrate a genuine interest in others. Your authenticity is key to everything.
- Promote a cohesive workplace. Reward those who actively engage.
- Avoid making snap judgments about others whom you may not even know. Don't take the bait about what employees tell you about other employees they may or may not support or even like.
- Support each generation's values and traditions. We are one humanity.
- Accommodate employee differences whenever you can. Give people the resources they need to be successful whenever possible.
- Be flexible in your leadership style. Strictness only instills fear.
- Respect, reward, and honor competence, experience, willingness to learn, and initiative.
- Be the bridge that you expect others to be, keep minding the gaps—big and small.

Cross-generational Collaboration

Here are 10 simple questions that leaders can ask to bridge the gap and collaborate with all generations:

1. How do you like to be communicated with (verbal, written, email, voicemail, text message, Zoom, Skype, etc.)?
2. When you are recognized for a job well done, do you prefer private or public recognition?
3. What motivates you to be more productive?
4. Do you prefer a direct and straightforward approach or a collaborative approach?
5. What is your comfort level with technology? What are you willing to learn and tackle?
6. What programs are you familiar with and what is your comfort level?
7. What software do you want to learn and how can the company assist you in learning it?
8. What goals do you have and where do you want to be in six months and one year from today? What does your brightest, best future look like?
9. If you were running the company, what would you change? Why? How?
10. Do you have any cost-or labor-saving ideas that can help you to do your job more efficiently or effectively?

Asking these leading questions will assist you in understanding other's communication styles, goals for future development, and how people want to be recognized and appreciated.

Leaders who create meaningful, peak experiences with whom they work help relationships flourish and profits soar. It can feel like a long climb to the pinnacle of leadership success, but applying some of these tools on a consistent and regular basis will help you to reach the summit of your dream much quicker and easier.

Dear Leader is a book that I believe helps each leader become stronger, more confident and more self-actualized. In turn, this creates conditions for your workers that enable peak performance and more enjoyable experiences.

> **"EVERY GENERATION IMAGINES ITSELF TO BE MORE INTELLIGENT THAN THE ONE BEFORE IT, AND WISER THAN THE ONE THAT COMES AFTER IT."**
> —George Orwell

Generational gaps in leadership are a complex dilemma facing leaders globally. No, not everyone thinks like you, looks like you, believes what you believe, or acts like you. And isn't that grand? What makes us unique is that which makes us all beautiful. The cultural divide is a gift and really is the connective tissue of our lives.

When you begin to appreciate the diversity across multiple generations and cultures, you begin to slowly unleash the leader within. Take time to examine the one-of-a-kind traits, attitudes, and work styles of every generation. They are each rich within their own experience of life and business. Take time to communicate and coach one another. Remember, age is only how many times the earth has revolved around the sun in one's lifetime.

By becoming more aware of each generation's differences and gifts, we are better able to assist leaders to modify their messaging for maximum effect and greater purpose. This happens despite the task at hand or specific relationship taking place. Never believe that only your way is the right way. It is not.

■■■

In this chapter I have acknowledged the greater purpose of multi-generational workers. How did this chapter shift your mindset regarding the importance of making everyone feel valued and appreciated?

____

____

____

____

____

____

____

____

What do you see as the possibilities of multiple generations working together and sharing ideas?

How do you envision becoming the possibility and reality of all you've learned in this chapter? What specifically will you do to improve your leadership in this area?

Next, let's dare to soar. This is a term I sometimes use when I refer to brilliant coaching. Let's get started.

CHAPTER 5:

Coaching for Success: Dare to Soar

The role of coach should be taken seriously. Those who aspire to it should begin by establishing positive behavioral characteristics and competencies that will set employees up for success and greater fulfillment and help people to soar to the next levels. Coaching is about helping others to rise higher. Coaches help their people soar. All leaders coach.

Guidelines for Coaching Success

The following skills and behaviors are essential for meaningful and long-lasting coaching to take place. My point is that coaching doesn't happen overnight. It builds. It takes time. It requires love and kindness, consideration, and an abundance of patience. I have put together this list of Guidelines for Coaching Success. Take time to review each suggestion and make notes on how you coach others and ways you would like to establish a positive and powerful coaching team. This list will help you create a structure for coaching success that you can customize for your culture and the personalities that serve the organization.

Share Knowledge

Freely and frequently share knowledge and expertise with others and then ask for the same in return. Coaching is a give-and-take proposition. Just because you are the manager or supervisor, does not automatically make you the only coach in the room. Employees coach too. They offer feedback and constructive ideas that improve the overall system. Listen closely.

Appreciate Differences

Respect and appreciate the differences in others and coach them accordingly. The basis of coaching starts with respect and trust. Without respect and trust, you have little to build upon. Let these two words be your guide. Start by respecting and appreciating everyone's differences. We are one humanity. Respect is our backbone. Respecting others allows us to coach with confidence and humility.

Trust Yourself and Others

Next, trust others, but mainly, trust yourself. People know when you trust them. They feel empowered and grateful. Trust builds confidence and speaks volumes about your coaching style. But even more importantly, as a leader, you must learn to trust yourself. Yes, you will make errors. Leaders are a work in progress and we are all flawed to some extent. As the leader, your best way to coach someone is to fail. That's right. I said fail. When you fail, you will want to share your mistakes with your team. This is true coaching to its very core. Celebrate mistakes—yours and others. Give people a chance to see that you are human and not a robot. Great coaches give of themselves from the heart. They don't pretend to be perfect. They strive to be human.

Solicit Suggestions

Encourage employee suggestions whenever change is being implemented. Every person at every level within your organization has something to contribute. That is what I call coaching in the moment. In my certification program on leadership, I discuss the different styles of coaching and the impact they all have. If you want to improve processes, teach people how to coach in the moment. Make it a safe environment for everyone to share an idea on how to improve the process. Coaching doesn't just happen at the top of an organization. It happens throughout the organization.

Enhance Understanding

Make sure people understand what is expected of them. Set boundaries and expectations. That is the secret sauce to greater coaching success. People cannot rise to the occasion if they do not know what is expected of them and the boundaries they must work within. Be transparent and share this upfront. You'll be a better coach for it.

Be Honest

Be up-front and honest with people at all times. Honesty and transparency rule the day. When you use this method as your compass, others will gladly follow and support you. People will ask for more of your coaching.

Communicate Openly

Communicate openly and honestly. My motto is that you tell the world who you are by how you communicate. I have traveled the globe and the way I connect with people from every walk of life is what sets the standard for my coaching practice. How do you tell the world who you are? Describe your coaching style here.

____

____

____

____

____

Stay Focused

Keep employees focused on the team's effectiveness and goals, and value personal contributions as well. Keep your eye on the ball. Don't let drama or disgruntled employees throw you off your game. Stay focused and you'll be a much more effective coach and leader.

Give Recognition and Appreciation

Give genuine praise and recognition for a job well done. In surveys done around the world, the number one motivator for anyone is knowing that their coach believes in them, their job is well done, and their efforts are appreciated. How do you demonstrate this as a coach? Be specific. Praise and recognition on a regular basis are key. Don't wait for an annual progress report to tell someone they are brilliant or appreciated. Do it today.

Help People Grow

Look for new ways to help others develop a person's full potential. Help people grow. Show them how to find their True North Star and move toward it. All you have to do is show someone how to reach higher.

Respect Others

Encourage team members to understand, respect, and support one another. No matter how good a coach you are, if your team is undermining one another or showing disrespect, your efforts are inconsequential. Respect, understanding, and supportiveness can be coached and taught.

Model Good Behavior

Walk the talk and model the standard of performance that is expected in others around you. You set the tone. You create the pathway to success and personal and professional fulfillment.

> **"A LIFE COACH DOES FOR THE REST OF YOUR LIFE WHAT A PERSONAL TRAINER DOES FOR YOUR HEALTH AND FITNESS."**
>
> —Elaine MacDonald, Canadian Activist

Understanding the Primary Leadership Styles of Coaching

There is not just one way or even a right way to coach. Instead, effective coaching can take on many styles, depending on the individual's personality and leadership style. We teach this in my certification program. It's very powerful.

The first step to take when training coaching as a leadership skill is to build awareness of the primary coaching styles that people use. Ask your leaders to describe their personal styles of leadership. This will enable you to match coaches with compatible learners in class, or help coaches adjust their styles as needed. Not every coach is meant to be with every learner or apprentice.

Dozens of different coaching styles exist, but I've chosen to focus on eight primary styles that people use most often. The objective here is to broaden the awareness and appreciation of these styles among your organization's leadership and then identify and relate to one or more styles.

Eight Primary Coaching Styles

Remember, not all coaches are the same, and coaches do not treat others the same. Instead, they recognize and appreciate the differences in each person they encounter. Coaching is a requirement for the successful and natural transition of our careers. Passing the baton becomes a reflection of all that we have become up to that moment.

1. **Key influencer.** A key influencer is usually a more dominant figure, a person who leads by example and who others aspire to emulate. This coaching style typically is practiced by people with tremendous influence and charisma. It's not a style for everyone, but it works for those who can deliver with confidence. Who do you know who leads this way?

2. **Formal and structured.** This style of coaching is seen in certain organizations. These organizations do a great job of coaching people through an established system that may include one-on-one support and an already-established system or process.

3. **Relaxed and informal.** This style of coaching typically works best with an experienced worker or colleague. Coaching like this usually means being available when support and guidance is needed. This coach is laid-back and usually takes an active role only when asked. His or her behavior is passive but meaningful. This can be a very powerful style of coaching as long as the receiver does not require too much personal attention.

4. **Hands-on.** If your mom or dad taught you how to fish, or how to cook a meal, or how to repair a broken item, or if someone showed you how to hail a taxi for the first time you visited New York City, you were coached hands-on. This style of coaching demonstrates

how to do something not easily learned from a book. Sometimes people refer to it as the coaching school of hard knocks or real-life learning.

5. **Hands-off.** This is sometimes referred to as coaching-on-the-go and might involve someone telling you where to find the information online or on YouTube, learn it yourself, and figure out the process. This is a great coaching style, but it is not for everyone. Some people require more hands-on coaching. It does, however, build self-assurance and self-reliance. The hands-off coach will be glad to help you after you've first tried to make a go of it yourself.

6. **Visionary.** This by far can be the most frustrating of all coaching styles. This coach sees the big picture and talks a great deal about his or her vision. This style of coaching can leave employees without any specific directions. The visionary style of coaching has the greatest impact when the coach takes the time not only to describe the big picture but also checks to see that everyone understands just how that big picture will be painted. Dr. Martin Luther King, Jr. did this extraordinarily well during his famous *I Have a Dream* speech.

7. **Group or team.** Team coaching is a different style of coaching but tremendously effective because people are held accountable in front of their co-workers and colleagues. This type of coaching takes place when an entire group or team of people band together to support one another and set goals. By sharing individual goals with a group of people, you're telling others what you intend to accomplish. Because this group revelation adds layers of accountability to follow through, employees tend not to give up or back out of their commitments. They've told everyone their goals, and they won't want to lose credibility.

8. **Stranger on the train or a coach in disguise.** The most influential coaching experience of your life can show up in ways and at times you don't even recognize. It may only occur once. Typically, it happens when you're least expecting someone to influence you. Perhaps you're sitting in the train station waiting for your train when a stranger sits down beside you and shares some information that changes the course of your life, or turns out to be extremely beneficial a month later. You may never see this coach again, but he or she leaves you with a lasting impression. This is sometimes referred to as *the stranger on the train* experience.

Not all coaches are found where you expect them. A great coach can be found on the internet; through a friend's referral; in online newsletters, magazines, or blogs; in books and trade journals; in organizations, churches, and clubs; and among your peers.

One of the most important aspects of coaching is what I call the Teach-Back, where a coach explains a concept, then has the recipient "teach" it back to the coach. This method solidifies the understanding of the new material and invites questions and correction into the process.

Teach-Back is common among the ongoing process of peer coaching. It can be the pinnacle of team building. You can partner new employees with people who possess the strengths and savvy to create shadowing programs where a new person can follow and learn from a seasoned and experienced worker. Partners can rotate as time moves along. You can set up specific Teach-Back sessions where people can teach back to others what they have learned. When we teach what we know, that is when we can claim the title of coach.

> **"IT TAKES SOMEONE WITH THE VISION OF THE POSSIBILITIES TO ATTAIN NEW LEVELS OF EXPERIENCE. SOMEONE WITH THE COURAGE TO LIVE THEIR DREAMS."**
>
> —Les Brown, Motivational Speaker and Author

Coaches impact eternity because there is no telling where their influence will extend. Great leaders learn to coach others. Our coaching skills come from our own life experiences. Who has been your most influential life coach? What did you learn? As we begin to shift our mindset on coaching and the possibilities of what coaching can provide, take a moment to reflect on the most influential coach in your life.

Who was your coach? What was his or her relationship to you?

____

____

____

____

____

____

____

____

____

How did this person coach others? What made your coach so effective? Describe your experience here:

____

____

____

____

____

____

____

Select a memorable time this person coached you and describe what you learned from the experience.

____

____

____

____

____

____

____

How did this coach communicate with you? What was his or her most valuable and constructive feedback?

____

____

____

____

____

____

____

What did you learn? What long-lasting impression did this coach leave on you?

____

____

____

____

____

____

____

What interpersonal skills or techniques can you take away from this coach and use now in your leadership position?

____

____

____

____

____

____

____

Are you ready to soar, dear leader? This chapter is meant to help you sculpt your own coaching style. The possibilities are endless. And as a stronger, better coach, you'll be prepared to turbocharge your team's performance and productivity, which I cover in the following chapter.

CHAPTER 6:

Turbocharging Team Performance and Productivity

> "IT'S NOT AS MUCH ABOUT RETAINING PEOPLE AS IT IS ABOUT ATTRACTING, DEVELOPING, AND NURTURING TALENT ALONG THE WAY."
>
> —Dr. Sam Adeyemi

As a leader, it's on you to pave the way for your team's success. And just a reminder, a position does not make you a leader; it only gives you the opportunity to lead. The most influential people in a workplace may not be those occupying the C-Suites. Anyone can be a leader when they use their gifts and skills to add value to people's lives.

Leaders take responsibility for their team's successes and failures, and I believe all of us would prefer to be part of a successful team than not. Winning teams perform well together and hit their goals efficiently. It's an added win if people enjoy their work environment, which shows in their productivity and morale. People thrive when they are part of a team where the leader sets a positive tone by being curious, positive, respectful, trustworthy, encouraging, and visionary.

You can have a team of the most intelligent and skilled people, but if their motivation is lacking or morale is low, it will drag down their productivity and performance. External factors like training or resources are issues you can influence as a leader. Communication and building a culture of respect, growth, and innovation are also variables you can control. The most successful leaders develop and nurture the skills and talent of those around them, key ingredients in maintaining performance.

You will have countless opportunities to influence others as a leader. The workplace's problems and challenges of your environment become your chance to influence others for good if you make a shift in not only your mindset but also the mindsets of your team. Human nature is complex. Sometimes people do not know why they behave the way they do. We can access power beyond human ability for them and for others. We can pull down mental strongholds. Anyone who has experienced a change of mindset knows that changing your thinking is almost like warfare. You can influence their concept of and expectations from leadership in order to motivate performance and productivity. There is no growth without personal improvement, and people will not experience sustainable progress without a change in their thinking.

Let us begin with interpersonal interactions and building relationships, both necessary and fundamental to growing performance.

> **"IMPROVED PRODUCTIVITY MEANS LESS HUMAN SWEAT."**
>
> —Henry Ford

Building Positive Relationships

It is said that a fish rots from the head. This means that as a leader, you set the culture for your team and for your workplace. Remember that employees don't leave jobs, they leave leaders.[3] Leaders maintain energy in the workplace by being enthusiastic about their goals and mission, and they are the ones who set the stage for success and maximum performance. If the leader is not passionate, team members will also follow that lead.

Building positive relationships in the workplace has everything to do with successful leadership, entrepreneurship, and coaching—and it all begins with you. Relationships set the atmosphere and culture of your workplace, and when relationships are strained, the leader is responsible for offering solutions and workarounds. Good leaders do the work to model the change and behaviors they wish to see in their workplace. They lead by example and set the tone and culture for the relationships.

Outlook and attitude are the key differences between the people who fail and the people who do not. Many organizations have endured seasons of struggle before they were able to set their systems on sound principles. In every instance, some people provided strong leadership and challenged the people to be positive. As a leader, you must be an incurable optimist, and your optimism must be contagious. All things are possible to those who believe.

---

3 Jack Kelly, "People Don't Leave Bad Jobs, They Leave Bad Bosses: Here's How to Be a Better Manager to Maintain and Motivate Your Team," *Forbes*, November 22, 2019, https://www.forbes.com/sites/jackkelly/2019/11/22/people-dont-leave-bad-jobs-they-leave-bad-bosses-heres-how-to-be-a-better-manager-to-maintain-and-motivate-your-team/?sh=3c920a3f22b9.

There is an understanding that you do not have to become friends with everyone you work with; chances are you will not—you should count yourself fortunate if do. Interpersonal relationships in the workplace are key to working on a team, achieving your objectives, and getting your job done with excellence. Working together with mutual cooperation and respect are critical to achieving your objectives and building strong performance.

The foundations of building such strong and positive relationships are trust, respect, self-awareness, inclusion, and good communication, among others. An atmosphere of trust tells people they are in a safe space that welcomes new ideas, collaboration, and creative action. Everyone is welcome to speak their peace without fear of retaliation, retribution, or rebuke. Such poor behavior is not welcome; however, open and civil exchanges always are. Mutual respect is the underlying current of all positive relationships, ethical behaviors, and communication exchanges, and should permeate the workplace. Strong teams also have members who are self-aware, take responsibility for their words and actions, and are sensitive to and curious about those around them. And because trust is established, team members can admit mistakes and take action to course correct when they happen. All contributions are valued and appreciated in an inclusive workplace because every viewpoint comes from a person's unique life experience. Finally, good communication depends on all these preceding attributes, and is vital to the success of your team.

> **"MOST OF US SPEND TOO MUCH TIME ON WHAT IS URGENT AND NOT ENOUGH TIME ON WHAT IS IMPORTANT."**
> —Stephen R. Covey, Author and Speaker

The power of positive relationships has the capacity to make or break your team, and setting that atmosphere begins with you. When we build positive relationships, we automatically become coaches and mentors for life. We build the capacity to become more productive and achieve greater results on the job. We alter our environment, making it more enjoyable—a place where everyone is genuinely excited to be part of the team and proud of the work they are doing.

Following are three influential items you should keep in mind when you're in a leadership role.

Create and Build a Trust-Oriented Workplace

How employees perform depends on a multitude of factors, many of which you as a leader control. You can help your team engage productively by encouraging a trustworthy culture that includes opportunities for professional growth, feedback, support systems.

Be honest. Bad or difficult news is not like fine wine; it does not improve with age. As hard as sharing unpleasant news can be, leaders bear this responsibility. You control the narrative and the timeline when delivering messages; avoiding or procrastinating only invites uncertainty and fuels the rumor mill. Model leadership by starting the conversation no matter how uncomfortable you may be. People tend to respect authentic, trustworthy leaders who tell the truth.

Show appreciation. People want to be acknowledged for a job well done. Showing sincere appreciation for people's efforts builds a positive workplace culture that values its people and fosters an environment of trust.

Empower people. Trust people to do the job you hired them to do, and provide them with the tools they need. They'll feel confident and energized. Micromanagement is the opposite of empowerment.

Actively listen. When communicating, make sure you're actively listening to what your team has to say. Paraphrase what you've heard to ensure you're receiving the message accurately and without judgment. Give everyone an opportunity to be heard.

Create a positive and supportive culture. When people feel like their contributions are valued and they have job satisfaction, they often perform better. Encourage free exchanges of ideas and information without fear of criticism. Creating a supportive work environment shows your team you not only care about the big picture, but also the painters of that picture.

Model the behavior you wish to see. To maintain team performance and productivity, you cannot assume your team automatically respects and values your leadership. You must demonstrate your ability every day by holding yourself accountable to the same high standards you have for others. This is easier said than done when you also have other responsibilities and deliverables that vie for your attention regularly, but it is no less important. You must demonstrate tone and behavior through your actions.

Communicate with purpose and consistency. How you communicate is just as important as what you communicate. Tap into your emotional intelligence and self-awareness when explaining goals, roles, and expectations. Communicate with the intent of getting it right, not necessarily being right. Ask questions when you are not sure.

> "PRACTICE RECRUITING YOUR PEOPLE EVERY DAY, EVEN THOUGH YOUR TEAM IS ALREADY ON BOARD."
>
> —Dr. Sam Adeyemi

Embody Positivity, Kindness, and Respect

Mothers throughout the whole world have told their children if they don't have something nice to say, don't say anything at all. This sage advice should be applied to the workplace, too. Kindness is a universal quality that is helpful in every interaction you have in your life. Benefits include helping others (and yourself) feel good, reducing tension, increasing morale, and lowering burnout. The biggest benefit of kindness is that it helps to fill the human need for social connections. Consideration for other people helps us connect with them and solidifies interpersonal relationships.

A *Harvard Business Review* article said, "When leaders and employees act kindly towards each other, they facilitate a culture of collaboration and innovation."[4] Your return on investment from an act or word of kindness can ignite a downstream of positivity. When showing

4 Ovul Sezer, Kelly Nault, and Nadav Klein, "Don't Underestimate the Power of Kindness at Work," *Harvard Business Review* (May 7, 2021), https://hbr.org/2021/05/dont-underestimate-the-power-of-kindness-at-work.

kindness, for example by praising a new idea or a job well done, you are making the effort to emphasize the positive in what you say, see, and do. By reaching out to others with genuine sincerity and authenticity, you are demonstrating that you not only care about what is happening in the workplace, you show an interest in team members as individuals. These actions speak loudly.

■■■

I have a colleague who used to play the license plate game on long car trips, where she and her siblings would look for cars with license plates from all 50 U.S. states. Once they began looking, they would continually notice where all the cars came from throughout their entire trip. In business and in life (and in the license plate game), you get what you look for. It is called "selective attention" because our brains filter out all the other stimuli so we can concentrate on what we're looking for. When you continually look for the positive in people and situations, you will notice it. Conversely, if you constantly seek out the negative, you will find that, too. An interesting way to look at this is if you are busy focusing on the negative things that happen, you might miss the good and positive things too.

The same goes for your workplace. You can guide your teams into seeing the positives. Be on alert for drama and don't feed into it by perpetuating or tolerating it; find the root and then do something about it. Instead of ruminating on a failure, use it to teach for the lesson in the experience. Take the difficult issues for what they are and make the choice to be the person to look for the learning opportunity and the chance for growth.

> **"DON'T ATTEMPT TO FIND THE MISTAKES. LOOK FOR THE GOLD."**
> —Dr. Sam Adeyemi

Redirect Negative, Hurtful Energy with Your Words and Actions

When you notice the rumbles of discontent creeping into your team, you must confront it head on. Problems are like a slow leak that perpetuate rot—and they do not go away on their own. You must take action to redirect situations that go sideways. You do not want a small issue spinning into a larger problem that affects your team negatively or destroys morale and workplace culture. Redirecting is a smart and positive way to be a forward-thinking leader.

In order to influence others around you, you must again look within yourself. Growth comes from within you, and so does your ability to manage any negative energy that affects your team. You must be willing to change and grow if you wish to improve. We often avoid tending to problems because we feel uncomfortable confronting a demanding or challenging issue. Difficult conversations are difficult for a reason—they make us uncomfortable and uneasy—but they are essential to keeping morale and productivity at a high level. Use times of discontent to solicit feedback from your team and look for answers to their problems and questions.

Find out the root of the issue that is causing the problem and then actively work to provide a solution. Was there adequate direction and communication on what the outcomes should be? Clarifying expectations should be your initial step of the conversation.

Empower others to offer their take on solving the issue. Use your skills of empathy and sincerity to authentically understand why negativity has entered the room, and then do something about it. A conversation is only awkward if you make it awkward. When you come at it from a position of curiosity, you will gain traction in the right direction. If you find you procrastinate or avoid confronting a challenge, look to a mentor, someone you trust, or hire outside professionals for their guidance and advice on how you can take action.

By demonstrating a positive and respectful attitude, you are showing you are willing to be uncomfortable and attend issues instead of ignoring them. Avoid trying to get people "back on track"—that's like trying to "fix" someone. It's almost insulting and about as effective as telling someone to "calm down." **A positive attitude drives passion—passion drives action—and action drives results.** Providing redirection is a positive way to take action with a caring attitude.

Morale and Productivity

Countless articles and studies have documented the influence of workplace morale on productivity and performance. Morale is thought of as the collective outlook employees have of an organization by way of their loyalty, enthusiasm, and sense of value and purpose. This outlook affects their attitude at work. When morale is high, productivity and team engagement tends to be high. Employees are engaged and work better in teams, resolve challenges and conflicts faster, and have a high sense of belonging and value. Good morale ensures long-term productivity. However, when morale is low—well, that is when things tend to take a turn for the worse. People feel unappreciated and unrecognized, and the organization can experience high absenteeism and high turnover. The workplace sees more conflict, increased dissatisfaction, and even a toxic work environment.

Why is this? What is the connection between morale and productivity? Multiple factors can negatively affect morale—poor communication from leaders, the nature of the work itself, unfair compensation or promotions, lack of work-life balance, and job insecurity, just to name a few. Conversely, high-morale organizations tend to have supportive, emotionally intelligent leadership who understand the value of work-life balance, invest in their employees, and support a positive internal culture. In most cases, high morale may lead to more productive workers.

High morale begins with strong leadership, whereas poor leaders lower employee morale. Number one reason for high morale is when you lead by example. People take their behavioral cues from their leaders. When leaders are disengaged, employees tend to feel undervalued and underappreciated. But when leaders are involved in day-to-day activities, you show your team that you are engaged and care about the work they are doing. Leaders who are empathetic praise and give credit where appropriate and show an interest in how their teams are feeling. And leaders who invest in their teams encourage professional and personal growth while showing they care about people's individual success.

Generational Knowledge

In chapter 4, we discussed the multi-generational workplace in general. We are discussing this topic a little deeper in this chapter because the relevancy is so critical to leadership standards today. Now, here's a breakdown.

Many differences exist between the generations in today's workplace, none so wide as we have seen between the 20th and 21st centuries. In fact, technological advances have been so great between the Traditionalists and Generation Z that it has essentially created two distinct life experiences. Distinctions in beliefs, thoughts, and actions among these generations is known as the "generation gap."

Did you know that this is the first time in the history of the American workforce that five different generations are working side-by-side (with the newest and youngest generation trailing right behind them)? In addition, we have a very diverse, inclusive, and global workplace. Intergenerational leadership and work ethic styles and differences are just now catching up to the generational and cultural preferences of people in the workplace. There has never been a more important time to mind the gap and better understand human behavior, because the responsibility of maneuvering such a diverse workforce falls on you as a leader.

Being a successful leader means knowing how to build bridges and then move your team over them. It also means bridging gaps whenever it is required. Building strong relationships is an art and often helps bridge gaps between leaders and their teams.

The following are generally understood generational groups of workers. Although the years may vary and overlap somewhat, the consensus of each generation remains consistent.

- Traditionalists (1922–1945): Known as a blend of the Greatest Generation and the Silent Generation, this generation is known for emphasizing the rules, hard work ethic, and trusting the government

- Baby Boomers (1946–1964): This post-World War II generation helped shape subsequent generations and came of age during the Vietnam War era; anti-war and anti-government
- Generation X (1965–1980): A generation of "latch-key kids" because of dual-income parents, this generation's characteristics include diversity, work-home balance, and a global mindset
- Millennials or Gen Y (1981–1996): Millennials and Gen Yers are known to be confident, have a sense of civic duty and are more entrepreneurial than preceding generations
- Generation Z (1990s–2010s): This generation has large virtual networks and uses social media to find jobs
- Generation Alpha or Generation Next: Not quite ready for the workforce is the next generation that popular media typically calls this demographic cohort that will succeed Generation Z. The ending birth years are late 2020s, and they'll be the newest generation of people entering the workforce.

As a global leader I've learned to keep my eyes open everywhere I go all over the world, because regardless of generation, people are people, and they have the same needs all over the world. In other words, I pay attention. When I travel to various countries, I watch the news and what I'm trying to do is identify the problems and the needs because I always want to be in the category of the people who solve the problems. In one of my keynote speeches, I mention that throughout my years traveling the world, my observation about humanity often comes down to two basic needs and feelings every beating heart desires: First is the wish for meaningful purpose. Every one of us wants meaning in our lives. Why do we get out of bed in the morning? What am I here for?

Second is that we all wish for a better tomorrow, whether that be for our children, our grandchildren, ourselves, or all of humanity. These two basic desires span the generations. We just want the world to be a better place after we leave it. Our multiple generations show us that we can all be better, and we can all do better. This motivates me personally to keep trying my best. What motivates you to do your best?

Building a Bridge to Human Performance

Building strong relationships bridges the gap between leaders and employees. Several strategies can assist in managing a multi-generational workplace. They are useful in any team but are especially so in multi-generational teams. You can boost communication, create a productive and safe working environment, and help your teams set goals.

By establishing multiple means of communication, you can bridge the generation gap. Strong leaders integrate the communication preferences of all generations. For instance, Baby Boomers tend to prefer face-to-face communication whereas Millennials tend to prefer electronic communications and Gen X and Y, prefer digital and beyond. To meet the diverse needs of a multi-generational workplace, you may need to share information in several formats, such as emails, ad hoc meetings, virtual meetings, etc., and follow-up several times to ensure your messages are received.

When you foster a flexible workplace environment that focuses on productivity, you are being considerate of how your teams and the individual people on them function best. Now more than ever with the onset of offsite workspaces, virtual meetings, and global office locations, flexibility is needed. Every generation as well as every person on your team has a preference on what factors influence them to produce excellence. What kind of environment does your team thrive in? What may work well for one person may not inspire another. One size does not fit all.

Creating a safe environment where everyone learns to adapt to different forms of communication while maintaining respect in the workplace is the mark of strong leadership. Encourage your teams to speak freely by creating a workplace culture that embraces all messages—the good, the bad, and everything in between.

Last, there's setting goals and expectations and communicating them clearly, the importance which I cannot emphasize enough. When your team has a clear understanding of what is expected of them, everyone should be united on their tasks and mission. By creating a structured progress that manages performance, teams have a tangible way of knowing when they are hitting (or missing) their marks, regardless of how they prefer to communicate or the environment in which they work. Structured processes become a way to reward teams when they've earned it, but they also provide immediate feedback when you need to make a course correction. You are guiding them on what to do, but they still get to choose how best to get the job done.

The more you understand different generations and how to bridge the gap, the more you appreciate and value all the differences and contributions each individual makes. Remember, you can't motivate people, but you can influence what they're motivated to do by serving as a bridge among generations.

In this chapter we've determined that the most successful leaders develop and nurture the skills and talent of those around them. These become the key ingredients in maintaining a turbocharged, high-performing workplace.

■■■

How did this chapter shift your mindset the way you build your teams and lead them?

What do you see as the possibilities for turbocharging performance as a leader where you work? Be specific.

How do you envision actually becoming these leadership possibilities when it comes to higher performance levels? What are your expectations of your teams' productivity over the next year? What makes you as a leader, the voice of reason?

Coming up, we'll discuss how to drill down on human behavior and branding for talent. What's your style when it comes to branding talent for the long haul of success?

CHAPTER 7:

Branding for Talent

You have undoubtedly heard of "branding" as it applies to your favorite product or service. You may favor some brands over others because of their reputation for quality, values, or ethics. Companies spend millions to strengthen and protect their brand, thereby securing their position in the market hierarchy and increasing their sales and profitability, but also to attract and keep top talent.

Have you ever thought how branding applies to your organization and your teams? Your organizational brand is your essence and your governing principles; it is the mark you not only leave on your product, but also current, former, and future team members. Empathetic and active leaders who invest in their brand to create smart, self-reliant, and innovative teams who are always striving to improve are the ones who will lead organizations in the future. These leaders know the value of a positive work environment and satisfied and fulfilled employees. Today's job market is incredibly competitive, and people want to work in an atmosphere that supports them as human beings, not just cogs in a colossal machine. The messages you send are vital to your survival as a business and your reputation as a leader.

Positive branding is fundamental to getting and keeping top talent in your organization, and as a leader, it's up to you to help your team prosper. You have to walk the talk to provide and maintain a positive working culture that lives its values and supports its team members on a professional and personal level. You can enhance or harm your brand through your messaging, actions, and intentions as a leader.

> **"TOO MANY COMPANIES WANT THEIR BRAND TO REFLECT SOME IDEALIZED, PERFECTED IMAGE OF THEMSELVES. AS A CONSEQUENCE, THEIR BRANDS ACQUIRE NO TEXTURE, NO CHARACTER AND NO PUBLIC TRUST."**
> —Sir Richard Branson, Virgin Group

The Marketplace, Like the Economy, Is Often Turbulent

Workers not only bring high-level skillsets to the workplace, they also bring higher and more demanding expectations. When this happens, the workplace often becomes more turbulent and intense. Potential workers are using every form of technology and every available social media tool to screen employers. Top talent is made up of savvy consumers—and they bring this discretion and focus to their job searches as well. The hiring game has shifted considerably.

This shift makes your organization's brand an essential part of your overall business and strategic plan. Traditional branding is no longer enough. Your company's brand has to resonate with consumers and workers, both inside and outside of the organization. It's then that your branding becomes the essential way you will attract and engage workers to join and stay as long as possible.

The goal is to match the right worker with the right employer and its culture at the right time. It's no longer about one business owner's ego or name recognition. It's now about the worker and his or her attraction to the brand they target as their next employer.

> **"A BRAND INCLUDES RITUALS, STORIES, AND RELATIONSHIPS THAT ACCOUNT FOR BOTH AN EMPLOYEE'S AND A CUSTOMER'S DECISION TO SELECT ONE PRODUCT OR SERVICE, OR ONE SPECIFIC EMPLOYER. THAT'S TRUE BRANDING FOR TALENT ON A BIGGER SCALE OF THINGS."**
>
> —Dr. Sam Adeyemi

Build Your Brand, Not Your Ego

There's a lot riding on your talent brand, because it is also your entrepreneurial mindset in many cases. And because you are in a leadership position, it falls on your shoulders to have a good understanding of its importance, and act accordingly to foster a strong and resilient atmosphere that welcomes innovation and supports your teams. I recommend these seven steps.

Step 1: Let Your Values Guide You

Do organizations have values like people? Sure they do. Leaders guide others by using their core values; organizations are no different. Much like your own personal values, an organization's values are its core set of beliefs—the "how" behind their "why." Values and missions differ slightly in that they both work hand-in-hand to create the backbone of your organizational culture, but whereas the mission says why your organization is heading in the direction it is, the values tell you how it will behave and treat others on the journey there. Values include governing principles, such as accountability, transparency, fairness, diversity, and responsibility; corporate philosophy, such as authenticity, empathy, and environmental stewardship; and basic guidelines or expectations of behavior for team members, such as inclusivity and showing up with positive attitudes.

Step 2: Be Authentic

Authenticity is a reflection of your entrepreneurial mindset. Without authenticity, your talent brand is as deep as a shallow puddle. People rarely leave organizations, but they do leave leaders. Potential team members want to know why others stay in your organization. By being an authentic leader, you show your team that you are the real deal, that you genuinely care about your team, and that you are willing to be their champion. When you hire for characteristic like "authenticity," you will see authenticity in your leadership as time goes on. As workers are promoted and move ahead, the traits you hired them for will surface in their teams, their levels of productivity, and inevitably your bottom line profits. The benefits to you and your organization can grow far and wide. Your branding reputation will begin to be known and respected nationwide and even internationally.

Step 3: Intergenerational Talent Is All Talent

Today's workplace has five generations of diverse and global people working alongside one another. We dive deep into this in our certification program. You can also review in chapters 4 and 6 in this book.

Each generation has a unique life experience to offer. The organizational brand should welcome each generation's viewpoint and actively work to accommodate different perspectives. You brought them onboard for a reason—for their talent, skills, perspectives, and creativity; it is all talent (even when it may look very different from person to person), and all talent should be valued by leaders. Embrace this and value what each person brings to work every day. Reflect what you expect.

Step 4: Set Up Everyone for Success

Create employee development plans to set everyone up for success, as I lay out in chapter 10. Remember, a brand is the "how" that takes you to the finish line and if you don't know where you're going, any path may take you there. A development plan outlines ways to help team members improve their skills in their current position and expand their knowledge in other areas and competencies so they'll be prepared to tackle bigger responsibilities in the future. The goal is to make this plan reasonable and attainable—something that can be achieved with dedication, hard work, and focus. It's your job to set every team member up for success, not failure, by shining a light on what they are good or what they love doing, and by continuing to build on past successes around those competencies. This dedication is reflected in your brand. Investing in team members' professional growth can help your brand stand apart from the pack by showing your commitment to learning and development.

Step 5: Focus on Talents and Strengths, Not Weaknesses

Be aware to shift your focus from finding weakness to promoting your team members' strengths, interests, and natural abilities. We experience more success by helping others expand their strengths and positive traits, rather than by highlighting or trying to eliminate weaknesses. Successful employee development plans focus on a team member's talents and strengths. They do not focus solely on a person's weaknesses and how to improve them. That's like teaching a fish to climb a tree—it's not going to happen because the fish is not built to climb. Challenges should certainly be addressed, but they should never be the primary focus for growing talent in an organization.

Step 6: Protect Your Brand by Protecting Your Talent

We know that people and their talent are our greatest assets. Long gone is the mantra "The customer is always right." Today, "Our people are our most valuable asset" is the more accurate corporate slogan. However, putting this into a daily branding practice can be challenging. Actively work to maintain your brand's integrity by activating organizational values to stay ahead of challenges. Keep a finger on the pulse of your organization and how current and former team members feel about your organization by monitoring social media and online employment sites. From there, you can enlist other leaders or team members to help promote or improve your brand by showing your positive attributes that make your organization a good place to work.

Step 7: Promote Team Members' Stories

Social media, blogs, vlogs, and job sites have the potential to showcase peoples' strengths and common interests outside the workplace, and it connects people on a human level. Humanizing your brand and its values can be a smart and cost-effective way to create authentic and effective goodwill. Microsoft did this through its blog, called Microsoft Life. Written by employees, it features stories about peoples' common interests outside the office, like family life, sustainability, inclusion, cooking, and community. Certain sections on an organization's website may also showcase employee talents and experiences. This is commonly exhibited in law firms, medical practices, engineering firms, and in technology-focused companies, which may produce content, services, or high-end product lines.

Use Values as Your Cornerstone

Earlier in this book I discuss the importance of values-led leadership. I also briefly touched on organizational values above. Core values and principles are not just an afterthought to enhance culture or manage human capital; rather, they are the cornerstone upon which the organization operates and leads, clearly defining its own unique character. Branding and values are tied together because they influence how you are perceived by others, including leadership, internal teams, and external customers. Just as your personal values guide your decisions, so do the values of an organization guide its actions. It is ideal when your personal values and principles align with that of the organization with which you work because you, in essence, are a values ambassador for your organization. Integrity, honesty, open-mindedness, dependability, reliability, among others, should be considered when guiding most decisions. Now is a good time to create your own list of important values that will help shape your organization's hiring practices, promotion opportunities, and succession planning. Invite input from your employees so that people experience stakeholder pride.

How an organization approaches everything it does and influences every interaction people have with it should be guided by its values, first and foremost. Values demonstrate an organization's character and personality, making statements of where it stands and what it believes in. Patagonia, Ben & Jerry's (now part of Unilever), Nordstrom, Harley-Davidson, Whole Foods, St. Jude Children's Research Hospital, Ritz-Carlton Hotels, Disney, and Southwest Airlines are brands known for their progressive values because they make a clear statement about who they are, what they do or produce, how they do it, and how they treat their teams. Values are the building blocks of your corporate culture, which in turn can influence team member morale, happiness, turnover, productivity, and job satisfaction.

Mission and vision statements can also help guide the process. They have separate outcomes for different reasons. Simple definitions of each include:

Mission Statement: This is who we are and what we stand for.

Vision Statement: Expresses the vision of what's to come, what the possibilities might be, and how we'll all get there.

By clearly communicating the values, mission, and vision your organization holds dear, you can encourage your teams to acknowledge their importance and then practice activating them. It all fits together and helps maintain a comfortable balance within the organization.

Careers offered within your organization should support and reflect your brand and image. Your approach can open the door for future and current employees to engage and rise through the ranks, setting higher standards and expectations for everyone.

How Performance Rankings Dilute Top Leadership Standards

Beware that performance evaluation rankings may work against you when it comes to branding for top talent. Performance rankings, especially when using numbers, can be degrading and deflating to employees. Consider providing performance reviews that offer measurements that focus on improvement, new ideas, revenues generated, commissions earned, and personal and professional growth. Many organizations in the past decade have dropped traditional numerical rankings when it comes to performance reviews. Whenever you assign a number to a person's performance, you risk the chance of ignoring the talent they actually bring to the table, which can be demoralizing. This can be in direct conflict with your talent branding efforts.

The key to branding for talent is to hire the right people for the right job at the right time. That's the secret sauce. When you marry these three steps, you'll be off to a great start. Remember that every organization, no matter what the economic marketplace may be, needs to have the best people who are engaged in making hearty contributions. Become a magnet for attracting and engaging the best talent. Never hire the best of the worst because you're short-handed on staff or growing too quickly to fill positions. Use creativity, generosity, sustainable values, and a welcoming environment of support to attract top talent. You'll be glad you did.

■■■

How did this chapter shift your mindset about branding for top talent? What will you do differently going forward? How would you describe your organization's brand right now?

What do you see as the possibilities for attracting the best of the best, instead of the best of the worst? Provide details.

How do you envision becoming a top talent recruiter and developer of new talent? How might this affect your succession planning program?

____

____

____

____

____

____

____

____

____

____

Along with branding to attract top talent, I believe imagination and fresh ideas are the key to sustainable leadership. Chapter 8 examines this area in more depth.

Part Three

CHAPTER 8:

Universal Laws of Imagination, Innovation, and New Idea Development

Think back to when you were a child and let your imagination run wild. What limitations did you place on your play? None, I would imagine. It probably never occurred to you to do so. You may have pretended to travel to distant lands or times, or invented new games to play with other children. With zero limits on your imagination, you could go anywhere or be anyone or do anything. Once you grew into the adult that you are today, did you begin to place limitations on your imagination? Do you dismiss your good ideas because you do not have the resources, time, or drive to make them a reality? Maybe reality crept in and implementing those ideas led to them dying on the vine. Or maybe someone else has told you multiple times that your ideas do not matter.

> **"IMAGINATION IS EVERYTHING. IT IS THE PREVIEW OF LIFE'S COMING ATTRACTIONS."**
> —Albert Einstein

Help Your Team Find Their Imaginative and Innovative Capacities

Unbridled imagination is the secret ingredient to all successful endeavors, from hand-held tablet computers to self-driving cars and beyond. All projects began as an idea. When you are in a leadership position, it is up to you to help those on your team find their imaginative and innovative capacities, and keep the creative ideas coming. It is your job as a leader to help others by nurturing and sustaining a supportive atmosphere that embraces change and builds upon common values. Imaginative leaders see the potential far beyond the here and now and encourage open dialogue to move those good ideas from imaginative thoughts into concrete reality. Innovative thinking can add value or lead to gains, continuous improvement, or rethinking new ways to do old things.

The Power of Imaginative Leadership

Envisioning a successful future is a powerful thing, but those ideas need to be acted upon to become a reality. Recognizing the power of imagination, innovation, and idea generation is the first step in a journey of growth and change. And in order to realize such a successful future, the atmosphere in the present must be one accepting of the creative process. Imagination solves problems, helps you overcome hurdles, thinks new ways around old processes. In a way, imagination helps you reverse-engineer an issue—by asking "what's the end game?" you can envision a solution and create a way to get there.

Among the many important facets to being an imaginative leader are vision, communication, and commitment. Great leaders practice all three. By adding love, core values, and curiosity to the mix, you can propel your team to launch their creativity and grow in value.

These elements all work together; when one element is missing, ideas may remain unrealized and unfulfilled.

Leaders who support creativity and innovation trust that their teams can not only come up with good ideas, and empower their teams to make decisions to realize those ideas.

Innovation as a Collective Pursuit

In my neighborhood, I've seen schoolchildren playing sports and encouraging one another to keep going and to do their best, celebrating each other for a job well done. I thought to myself that somewhere along the road to adulthood, that collaborative spirit vanishes and is replaced by competition. These same children grow up and enter workplaces where people compete, not collaborate, within their own teams. Their ability to come up with and share new ideas seems to fizzle out on their journey to growing up and fitting in with their peers.

Much like a seed grows into a tree that bears fruit, innovation grows in an environment that is nurturing and supportive. Innovation is contagious and inspiring. A good brainstorming session may even spark many new ideas—some that never would have surfaced had it not been for the conversation in the first place! Brainstorming is a fun part of the curriculum in my leadership certification program.

To innovate, it is helpful to have more than one mind, one opinion, one idea. It is a collective pursuit. Innovation is not a solitary activity—it requires many great minds working together creatively to solve problems and achieve lasting change. Sharp leaders value creative thinking on their teams. Here are some considerations for you to ponder:

Set the stage for innovation. New ideas can come from anyone—from frontline workers to C-Suite executives—and all ideas should be considered and welcomed. You never know where you are going to find the next big innovation. This very minute it could be bubbling in the mind of one of your colleagues. But how would you know if you don't set the stage of an open-minded environment that welcomes new ideas? This is the first step—cultivating an environment that welcomes new idea development and challenges conventional thinking, one where your team feels comfortable expressing their ideas with zero repercussions or retributions. This is part of the empowerment factor I discuss at length in this book.

Allow and encourage your teammates to execute those ideas, to wholly own them, and carry them out as they originally envisioned. Ownership of ideas empowers people and grows trust by signaling you have faith in your people. One of the greatest human desires is to know that someone believes in you. By establishing this sort of welcoming environment, you encourage future idea generation and innovation.

Take risks. When you are risk-averse, you embrace mediocrity, and that is the opposite of innovation. Taking a risk also means you are willing to fail, but if you think of failure as a great teacher, then you are already ahead of the game. Failure can inspire new and creative ways to solve a problem, and can show you ways not to do something, which also can be helpful. Supporting failure is actually rewarding the creative process, which should be encouraged.

Reward individual and team efforts. It is important to recognize people for their contributions and efforts. We all like to be acknowledged for our contributions and successes. If there are people on your team who naturally generate ideas that come to fruition, take a moment to recognize their individual efforts as you applaud the efforts of the team as a whole. Be aware that all team members may voice their ideas in different ways, and those on your team who are more introverted may express their ideas differently. You want recognition to be a positive morale booster for the entire team, not a demoralizing endeavor that only favors the outspoken. Recognition can go far beyond dollars; it can be a note of gratitude, a promotion or change of title, an afternoon off, or an experiential reward like a team outing, to name a few. Ask your team how they would like to be recognized. Their answers may enlighten you.

Micromanagement Stifles Innovation

Are you a micromanager? Do you need to know every detail of every interaction or task every minute of every day? That may be an extreme way of thinking about micromanagement, but my point is the same: when you micromanage your teams—when you make all decisions, excessively supervise, or overly criticize—you stifle their innovative spirit and creativity. People want to think for themselves, be empowered to make large and small decisions, and be free to work in the ways that best suit them. When people feel micromanaged, morale tanks and innovation sinks along with it. People create some of their best ideas on-the-fly so be sure to give them the freedom to think big.

Encourage Creativity, Imagination, and Intuition

Intuition is a leader's reservoir of vision, instinct, and creative genius. In the word intuition is its root form, or in Latin, meaning *to see,* to *imagine, to peer* or *look,* or *to picture.* Using your intuition as a leader can be extremely valuable, but it also takes practice and time to build your inner trust. In hundreds of interviews I have done with experienced leaders, as well as up-and-coming leaders, many acknowledged the value they place in their gut instincts, or intuitive talents. Albert Einstein once said, "The really valuable thing is intuition." I agree.

When leaders learn to trust their gut feelings, they also develop a keener perception and judgment in the workplace. Integrity and values-led leadership both stem from our deepest intuition about what is right and how best to treat others. As time goes on and with experience, we gain our own unique perspective on a variety of situations. We use our senses to experience our environment. Some of us travel the world. We all come from a variety of global cultures that instill belief systems, values, and ethics. It's the combination of all that input that helps us develop our inner vision and intuitive gut as leaders. This becomes our map of the world. How you choose to expand your map and step outside all that you've learned up to this point is now up to you.

In another book I wrote titled *Ideas Rule the World*, I express that it is our human ability to take relevant impressions, experiences, and comparisons and sift through them with ease. This helps us to arrive at conscious solutions as we approach each new challenge or problem. It's the essence of problem solving—finely tuned. It's smart thinking. In fact, I am quoted as saying, "Smart work yields better returns than mere hard work." Tapping into our creative self, our intuition, and our greater imagination speaks directly to this point. It's the triumph of all our ideas and feelings combined.

To gain greater understanding of your intuitive leadership abilities, creative talents and imaginative processes, take time to respond to the following statements and questions. Don't overthink your answers. Write down whatever comes to mind first.

Describe a time you relied on your instincts versus your actual training or experience. What occurred? Was the outcome a good one? How so?

____

____

____

____

____

____

____

When you have a hunch about something, do you follow up on it? What results have you had when you have followed through on an intuitive feeling? What results have you had when you did not follow your gut feeling about something? Be specific.

____

____

____

____

____

____

____

____

Do you tend to ignore your feelings, even when they are strong? Why do you think that is the case?

Do you consider yourself a creative thinker? Why or why not?

What creative ideas have you had lately?

How would you rate your creativity and imagination on a scale of 1 to 5, with 5 being the highest rating? How have you specifically applied your creative mindset or imagination when leading teams or solving workplace issues?

Name a person you admire who is exceptionally creative or intuitive. Why do you admire him or her? What lessons have you learned from this person?

Do you believe there is a connection between creativity, intuition, and good management, judgment, and greater wisdom? Why or why not? What specific connections do you see happening?

____

____

____

____

____

____

____

____

____

What global organizations do you see actively implementing imagination in the workplace? For example, Disney has an Imagineering division, where engineers come up with new ideas for their theme parks' rides and exhibits, animation, movies, and music. The department is specifically designed to encourage imaginative thinking, touching the human experience at what is called "The happiest place on Earth" and ultimately resulting in greater corporate success and profitability.

____

____

____

____

____

____

____

____

____

Intuiting as a Logical Process

After you respond to these statements and questions, take time to share your ideas with other leaders or your team. The point is to encourage other leaders, including yourself, to build awareness of intuiting as a logical process to act on. In doing so you will also learn to trust your inner voice of wisdom and find new ways to solutions when you feel lost or without direction. This is how to maximize your internal compass and become a stronger, smarter, better leader for the organization. I believe this book will help guide you in the process.

■■■

How did this chapter on fresh idea development and the universal laws of imagination shift your mindset and the way you will create and innovate going forward? What first steps will you take?

What do you see as the possibilities going forward? Can you name your own universal laws of imagination? Come up with three original ideas here:

____

____

____

____

____

____

____

____

____

How do you envision actually becoming the possibility of innovation and creativity as a leader? Be specific. Ask others for their ideas and record them here. Brainstorm with other leaders.

____

____

____

____

____

____

____

____

____

There's no doubt that imagination and innovation lead to better problem solving and decision making. Chapter 9 has some good pointers on these topics. Take a look.

CHAPTER 9:

Creative Problem Solving and Decision Making

Creativity is not just for artists or actors. It's for leaders, too. Everyone is creative in their own right. Think how dull leadership, or the world for that matter, would be without creative influence. We would not have self-driving automobiles, airplanes, flat-screen TVs, computers, space technology, smartphones, drones, smart watches, artificial intelligence, or robotic assistants. All these technologies were once just creative ideas that had the great capacity to change the world. Even a re-make of an old song is a creative endeavor because despite it using the same lyrics, a new voice, tempo, or beat makes it fresh and unique. All leaders can use a fresh coat of paint to revitalize and challenge old ways and outdated processes.

To achieve success in today's workplace, thinking creatively, implementing creative solutions with decision making power, and contributing innovative and thought-provoking ways to give all that we can are essential to your leadership growth and development. This is something we emphasize in our High-Impact Leadership Certification Program as well, using real-world tools and experiential exercises.

Creativity in the workplace can help boost your success because it gives you opportunities to innovate or challenge old systems with fresh ideas. New offerings and services sprout from not only outside-the-box thinking but expand and lift-the-box-higher thinking. Creativity keeps you ahead of your competition. When creative thinking is taught in the workplace it can be directly connected to profitability, higher performance levels, and employee engagement.

The problems we encounter on the job do not always have to be major issues. Every day, we face decisions; some have little implications whereas others have bigger impact. We run into challenges that require creative problem solving all day and every day, from when we wake up and decide what to wear (Is that shirt I wanted to wear clean?) to how to get to work (How do I get around this traffic jam so I'm not late?) to what to eat for dinner (Do I have enough vegetables in the refrigerator for a salad?) to how to get your toddler to go to sleep (I'm still figuring out that one, and my children are grown!). Good leaders make decisions big and small with creativity and confidence. When you apply your imagination, you can develop solutions you may not have otherwise thought of.

Keys to Problem Solving as a Process—Breaking It Down

Creative problem solving goes beyond brainstorming. It is a process with a beginning, a middle, and an end that breaks down a problem into smaller bits in order to understand it better, find ideas as possible solutions, then weigh those ideas to see which are the best fit. Many of us follow this process without consciously thinking about it.

Identifying a problem is the first step on the road to finding a solution. Make sure you identify the root of the problem and not a spin-off; for example, your laptop is running slowly. Is the computer itself faulty, or perhaps it just needs an upgrade in software? Identifying the "why" of your issue helps further clarify the scope of your challenge. A slow computer may derail your workflow but the real cause of your challenge is you are missing important deadlines because your computer fails to suit your needs. You must also consider what kind of outcome you are looking for.

Next, consider possible approaches to solving your challenge. As you brainstorm and generate possible solutions, research which solution best fits your needs. Get curious and explore by conducting online searches; asking friends, family, or experts about their experiences; or even go old-school and visit the library for in-depth answers. Using the laptop example further, you could research what kind of computer speed or programs are most helpful for your work, ask colleagues what kind of systems they use, and search for any current computer discounts. It's even helpful to take small breaks to step away from your brainstorming. It seems counterproductive, I know, but in some cases, even a little space away from concentrating helps solidify your thoughts. Unplug to plug back in. You'll find in many cases that you will hit a reset button for yourself that moves you forward faster.

Once you have several possible solutions, you will want to evaluate them. This can easily become your own customized internal metrics. Again, using the computer example from above, evaluate what the costs or possible consequences are? Do you purchase an expensive computer with cutting-edge functionality or do you merely need to update your operating system? Does your solution align with your original challenge? If it does not, it might be time to brainstorm some more.

Finally, you want to act on your solution. Creativity means little if action isn't part of the execution. This is where you do the work to solve your challenge.

> **"AVOID TAKING THE PATH OF LEAST RESISTANCE. DON'T ASSUME THAT WHAT WORKED YESTERDAY IS RIGHT FOR TOMORROW. BE PRESENT BUT THINK AHEAD."**
>
> —Dr. Sam Adeyemi

Tools to Help You Lead the Way Personally and Professionally

Mind Mapping and Brain Mapping

A mind map, sometimes referred to as a brain map, is a visual representation of your thoughts, ideas, and concepts, and how they connect to one another. The process applies to both your professional endeavors, as well as your personal activities. Creating a mind map can help you get your thoughts down in a creative and illustrative way.

Even if you are not a visual thinker, mind mapping and brain mapping can help you examine, create, understand, and remember new ideas. A mind map is both artistic and analytical and engages the creative parts of your brain because it helps you get your thoughts out so you can better reflect and organize them. The idea behind them is to make you a better thinker. That is where the magic really happens. Your mind map is as unique as you are! Get creative! Use colors, doodles, or whatever you need to express your words and ideas. Google mind mapping and see myriad alternative ways to approach this reliable and reputable process. There are numerous apps that provide this function, too.

You can use a mind map to help clarify your thoughts on anything—work, family, vacation planning, exercise, grocery lists, whatever you need to noodle out. Once you begin the practice, you may find it a fun way to help yourself problem solve and plan. I have a friend who uses this process for business projects, but also used it to plan her daughter's wedding.

Where to Start

How do you begin? On the center of your page, write or draw the main idea you wish to develop. The central word becomes the title, subject, theme, or can be just a thought you need to reflect on. Now, expand on the main idea by drawing lines for each subtopic, connecting the lines from the center toward the edge of your page. Continue to develop your subtopics by branching out the lines. Repeat this process with each subtopic. When you're finished, your map may look something like the image on the next page.

What Mind Mapping Can Do for You as a Leader

Mind mapping has often been referred to as a secret formula that often uses nothing more than colored pens, or an iPad or tablet, and your imagination. Mind mapping is known for helping leaders to express their ideas, solve problems in the workplace, and make life easier in general.

There is a lot of information on the internet about this process and many apps, too. My purpose here is to simply introduce you to the concept. It's an effective tool that can help you cut time in half and give you vision for a brighter tomorrow.

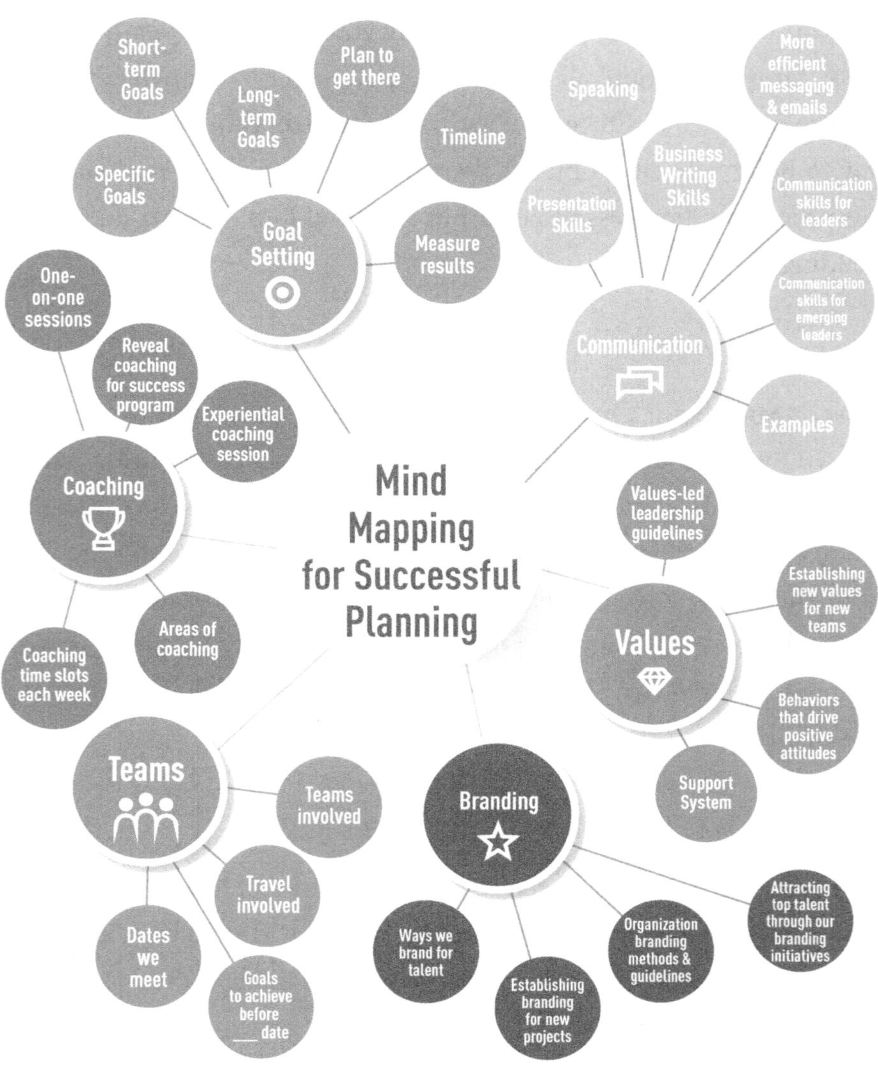
Mind Mapping for Successful Planning
Goal Setting
Short-term Goals
Long-term Goals
Plan to get there
Timeline
Specific Goals
Measure results
Communication
Speaking
More efficient messaging & emails
Business Writing Skills
Presentation Skills
Communication skills for leaders
Communication skills for emerging leaders
Examples
Coaching
One-on-one sessions
Reveal coaching for success program
Experiential coaching session
Areas of coaching
Coaching time slots each week
Values
Values-led leadership guidelines
Establishing new values for new teams
Behaviors that drive positive attitudes
Support System
Teams
Teams involved
Travel involved
Dates we meet
Goals to achieve before ___ date
Branding
Ways we brand for talent
Establishing branding for new projects
Organization branding methods & guidelines
Attracting top talent through our branding initiatives

Mind maps make it easy to come up with new ideas, brainstorm and find fast answers to your concerns. Everyone uses this process differently. There's no right or wrong method.

What Is the Purpose?

- A fun way for taking notes and jotting down ideas
- A unique way to revise ideas with simplicity
- A quick way to bring new ideas into your mind and break them down into specific pieces, projects, outcomes, and orderly deadlines

Mind mapping works because it is not considered boring or repetitive. It is a process that you make your own and you work the process as you think best, one step at a time. It is a fascinating way to blend our logical mind with our creative mind.

Now it is time for you to create your own mind map. Start in the center with an idea that is important for you to address or solve now. Then build out the structure of how you will make it happen.

Once you have created your visual mind map, list the resources and timeline it will take to make it happen. I've used this process and similar creative approaches when writing my books or creating new learning and training programs, like our certification program that supports this book's ideas. This simple process allows me to see the bigger picture, break things down in to bite-sized pieces and clearly identify the steps required to get me to where I am headed. I recommend you try it.

Chart or Diagram Your Options

Traditionally called a *flow chart*, a decision making chart or diagram can also be used to visualize the life cycle of an idea from brainstorming to action. You can use many different applications or software programs to help you process your path toward your preferred outcome. These tools also offer a visual breakdown of a challenge and possible solutions and outcomes. By asking yes or no questions, you plot a chart of possibilities.

By breaking down your challenge, you can then use a diagram to plot out your ideas. Start by setting a goal or writing your challenge; next, consider the stakeholders, budget, and risk you'll need to take and write the different possible outcomes for each; then compare the best alternatives and weigh the best choices; finally, monitor your progress after you take the big leap. Remember, you can always revisit your decisions if your choice does not work out in the ways you originally intended. A word of caution, though: sometimes the outcome can be a costly outcome; hence you want to weigh your alternatives and choices carefully from the onset so you get the best possible outcome.

Create a Decision Matrix

Creating a decision matrix is similar to charting or diagraming, but instead of using an "if-then" visual, you instead create a table. The rows of the table list the choices you should consider, and the column heads are the features for each choice you should consider. In each column, score the features on a scale of 0 (not at all) to 5 (must have). Next, you'll want to figure out the importance of each feature (assign a weight) to determine which is most important to you. Use the weight to multiply each score by the number you assigned as important to give you weighted scores for each possibility. Finally, add the rows and the highest number to show which choice you prefer.

Using the example of purchasing a computer from above, some of the features you might consider could be price, battery life, processor speed, time for delivery, and screen size.

Sample Decision Matrix

	Price Weighted Score	Battery Life/ Weighted Score	Processor Speed/ Weighted Score	Time for Delivery/ Weighted Score	Screen Size/ Weighted Score	Total Weighted Score
Weight of Importance	3	2	5	1	1	
Computer A	3/9	3/6	2/10	3/3	0/0	28
Computer B	0/0	0/0	1/5	1/1	3/3	9
Computer C	3/9	3/6	2/10	3/3	3/3	31
Computer D	2/6	1/2	3/15	3/3	0/0	26

Using a decision matrix, you can decide between all the options when each has different features worthy of your consideration. A weighted ranking system can help you determine which option is best. The example shows Computer C is the highest ranked option, and therefore your best choice.

Use the 80/20 Rule

Named for Italian economist Vilfredo Pareto, a Pareto analysis is the principle that 20 percent of factors contribute to 80 percent of the outcomes—or in other words, identifying which small factors have the biggest impact, either positively or negatively. As with the decision matrix, each benefit (or problem) is assigned a numerical score based on its impact; the higher the score, the greater the impact. A Pareto analysis can help you identify the root causes of a benefit or problem and prioritize which cause will yield the biggest bang for your buck. By assigning your resources to the issue that has the potential for the biggest effect, you can tackle issues in your workplace efficiently and strategically. Once you have the root cause identified, you can use other creative means to unearth solutions to either solve a problem or magnify a benefit.

For example, you know that 80 percent of your business comes from 20 percent of your customer base. If you used a Pareto analysis to isolate the characteristics of those customers, you can target your advertising and marketing efforts toward others in that same demographic. When you pinpoint the small changes that will make the biggest impact, you are thinking strategically and dedicating finite resources on what will advance your goals.

Four Ps Reframing Matrix

The Four Ps Reframing Matrix is another tool you can use to confidently make strong and appropriate decisions. This matrix takes different perspectives of multiple people into consideration, inviting numerous creative solutions to the party. Examine your issue from the following perspectives:

- **People.** Who is affected, what do they think, and what's in it for them?
- **Product.** Does your product currently fill the needs of your customers?
- **Planning.** Can you pinpoint any challenges or is there room to improve your offerings?
- **Potential.** Can you boost productivity or increase sales/morale/initiative?

Challenge or Need to Fill

Perspective 1 Issue #1 Issue #2 Issue #3	**Perspective 2** Issue #1 Issue #2 Issue #3
Perspective 3 Issue #1 Issue #2 Issue #3	**Perspective 4** Issue #1 Issue #2 Issue #3

What may be a home run solution from one perspective may be a strike out from another. It is important to consider perspectives other than your own when making important decisions.

SWOT Analysis

No list of decision making tools would be complete without adding a SWOT analysis. SWOT stands for Strengths, Weaknesses from internal factors and Opportunities and Threats from external factors. This tried-and-true tool for making informed decisions has been in existence for decades for good reason: it is easy to use and it is effective.

Internal	**Strengths** What do you do better than others? What do you have that the competition does not?	**Weaknesses** What do others do better than you? What can you improve?
External	**Opportunities** What trends or growth can positively affect you?	**Threats** What trends or growth can negatively affect you?

Transform Ordinary Thinking into a Think Tank Change Laboratory

Apply what you've learned to these possible real-life scenarios. Practice using the tools described above to creatively problem solve with the real-life categories below. This can be an enjoyable experiential exercise with your team or leadership group. Have fun with this! The more fun people have using this process, the more they will use it for building out all type of creative problem solving.

Work Situations	Home Life	Community Living
Holding performance reviews	Planning a party	Planning neighbor newsletter
Evaluating a new project	Helping kids with homework	Doing charity work
Hosting sales meetings	Planning a vacation	Recruiting volunteers
Planning retreats	Completing household chores	Volunteering
Holding management meetings	Doing weekly scheduling	Recruiting neighborhood watch
Finding solutions	Prioritizing financials	Forming childcare co-op
Resolving conflicts	Organizing your household	Planning political campaigning
Planning events	Resolving family conflict	Beautifying parks
Planning projects	Planning a wedding	Planning school carnivals
Performing budget reviews	Helping kids to "think"	Holding fund raisers
Holding leadership meetings	Getting organized	Planning church projects
Completing strategic planning	Doing home improvements	Planning holiday projects
Hiring and promoting	Landscaping and gardening	Performing city planning
Performing daily operations	Hosting a garage sale	Holding town meetings
Planning marketing	Selling existing house	Completing building planning
Planning company newsletter	Buying a new house	Planning school projects

Self-Assessment: Assessing Your Natural Creative Nature

We now know that whole-brain thinking is something all of us can implement with practice. It's the type of thinking that when we make the effort, we can benefit from both sides of our brains' power. However, there are still some preferential sides of the brain that tend to dominate our approach to creative thinking and problem solving. Take a moment to evaluate whether you believe you are on occasion more influenced by the left side of your brain (logical and analytical), or by the right side of your brain (creative and innovative). Respond by circling *Agree* or *Disagree* after each statement.

Statement		
1. I am happiest when I am free to make the final decision about what should be done.	Agree	Disagree
2. I trust my instincts and rely on my gut feelings, even when provided information to the contrary, before making a final decision.	Agree	Disagree
3. I enjoy visiting new places and foreign countries, and trying new things.	Agree	Disagree
4. I have a difficult time making decisions without all the facts.	Agree	Disagree
5. I read all of the information available to me before a meeting or before introducing a new idea.	Agree	Disagree
6. I prefer a logical approach to solving problems. It feels most comfortable to me.	Agree	Disagree
7. I'd rather someone make a formal presentation in a meeting, rather than just spontaneously throwing out ideas and suggestions to problems or challenges.	Agree	Disagree
8. I like brainstorming better than taking a structured approach.	Agree	Disagree

9.	I observe things going on around me and factor that into how I feel about something.	Agree	Disagree
10.	I really don't pay attention to what's happening around me, unless someone calls my attention to it.	Agree	Disagree
11.	I am very organized.	Agree	Disagree
12.	I am more visual than auditory when processing information.	Agree	Disagree

Explanation of Self-Assessment

First, know that there are no right or wrong responses to this assessment.

Everyone has a unique style of processing information. Some of us are more left-brain oriented (linear and logical) in our thinking and some are more right-brain oriented (imaginative or visual). But actually we can develop both equally with practice. Yes, some people use both sides of their brain almost equally. The goal is to work both sides of your brain and strike a comfortable balance between both logical and creative thinking whenever possible. When we do this, we help ensure that we will make fuller, more satisfying, even better decisions and as a result become more well-rounded in our approach to life's ever-evolving issues and demands. This is why developing our creative muscle is so critical for leadership.

If you agreed to statements 1, 2, 3, 8, 9, and 12 you have indicated in these areas that you may be slightly more right-brain oriented and enjoy a creative and innovative approach to problem solving. If you agreed to statements 4, 5, 6, 7, 10, and 11, you have possibly indicated that you are a bit more left-brain driven, preferring a more logical and analytical approach to things at times. Of course this is all relative and subjective. But it's great information for vigorous leadership brainstorming sessions.

The Creative Process of Stand-Up Comedy

Comedy clubs are very popular, especially in major U.S. cities. They fill a gap for spontaneity and a break from everyday life with dinner, drinks, and the chance to laugh out loud. Here's a fun fact. Did you know that when a comedian tells a joke, the audience tends to make assumptions about what is going to happen next in the story?

The comedian knows this upfront obviously and, therefore, has to set up a creative process for joke telling. He or she realizes that the people are assuming something about the story and its ending, and so the comedian, or storyteller, purposely uses a "punch line" to destroy the audience's perception or assumption. The diversion from what the audience thinks would be next is what makes it funny.

This is all thought out ahead of time and is delivered in a way that makes the audience laugh. This is called a creative process and explains why everyone is not cut out to be a standup comic.

Why do you think timing is important in this process? How have you applied a creative process, with humor, on the job, or in meetings? How would you describe your creative process?

> **"BYPASS YOUR ASSUMPTIONS AND THINK CREATIVELY. DON'T BE CONSTRAINED BY OLD RULES."**
>
> —Dr. Sam Adeyemi

With creative decision making in place, we can activate our imagination at the same time we face choices. When we combine these traits in leaders, we'll surely be carried away to opportunities never before realized. Without creative thinking and problem solving programs for future leaders, there could be a dead end to many remarkable projects. Creativity is the fuel that can bring all of us to new worlds and new possibilities.

■■■

How did this chapter shift your mindset regarding creative problem solving and decision making in your company or as a leader?

What do you see as the possibilities for better, faster, more impactful decision making on the job?

____

____

____

____

____

____

____

How do you envision actually becoming a better decision maker and problem solver? Can you provide one example below? Which of the processes outlined in this chapter are you most willing to try? Why?

____

____

____

____

____

____

____

All right, you've got nine chapters under your belt. We're in the home stretch. Next comes the creation of your personalized leadership development program. This becomes your plan of action for all we have covered so far. Let's get moving.

Part Four

CHAPTER 10:

Personalized Leadership Development Planning

We can no longer simply depend on traditional career development or business-as-usual leadership development courses we once relied upon. Global talent is just that—it is global. Leaders rise up from all corners of the world and come in all shapes and sizes. Personalized and individualized leadership development is the key to long-term success and growth—growth within the organization and growth within the hearts and minds of your aspiring leaders. This book and the accompanying certification and training program will help you to build stronger leaders synergistically. As we create more impactful, in-person and virtual leadership development opportunities, this book will become your daily field guide for developing effective talent, from Dubai to Denver and beyond.

Consider this book and the certification program that supports its teachings as a user-friendly guide and also a companion for you and your teams as you navigate the often delicate process of individual leadership development planning.

Harness the Power of Leadership

Our employees' ultimate success is often a reflection on how well leaders have developed their potential and talent up to that point. People often grow beyond anything we could have imagined for them, and we may never know where our influence stops. This is what is most exciting about leadership—its far-reaching effects.

In order to be able to develop people to their greatest level of potential and performance, we have to relinquish our power and let the learner take the lead. It is our job to facilitate the success of others. It is the employees' responsibility to be their own mentor and make things happen in their own way and with their own flair and style. We all make the journey together.

Leadership development planning is similar to going skydiving. Both require leaps of faith. In this metaphor, the aspiring leader is the skydiving student and the leader is the skydiving instructor. The parachute is the leadership development plan. How pretty the parachute is or what color it is means nothing if that parachute doesn't open and function for a smooth landing at the end. Leadership development plans, like parachutes, have to be sturdy, substantive, reliable, strong, flexible, real-world, user-friendly, easy to navigate and manipulate, and able to steer to the ultimate career drop zone.

Your ultimate objective is to provide each and every aspiring leader with the best tools and resources available to help ensure a successful career flight and safe landing.

What Is an Employee Development Plan?

Aspiring leaders who have demonstrated certain talents and stability are usually hardwired for success—provided they have a plan to follow. A leadership development plan is a written strategy that provides the individual with a step-by-step process that will help the person to achieve his or her career goals—both short-term and long-term. The plan's purpose is to develop the employee's strengths to his or her greatest levels of talent and competency, achievement, and greater potential. We lift up those around us. A personalized leadership development plan is also sometimes called a career development plan, individual development plan, or career-pathing strategy. You'll come across many terms for the same process.

Leadership development plans include the perspectives of both a supervisor or manager and his or her team members. The goal is to make the plan reasonable and attainable, something that the employee can achieve with dedication, hard work, and focus. It does not have to be complicated. It's actually very straightforward in design and development. It's your job as a manager or supervisor to set every employee up for success. We set people up for success when we let them shine at what they are good at, work at what they love doing, and continue to build a track record of success around those competencies and capacities. Developing leaders is not about improving on weaknesses. It's about enhancing an individual's strengths and strongest abilities.

How Focusing on a Person's Weaknesses Can Backfire

The most helpful leadership development plan focuses on a person's talents and strengths. It does not shine the light solely on the person's weaknesses and how to improve them. Weak areas and challenges are certainly discussed and covered, but they are not, nor should they ever be, the primary focus for growing talent in an organization. The plan may backfire if you do.

Weaknesses and special challenge areas of each person can and should be discussed and then neutralized in an individual leadership development plan, thereby making way for and allowing the employee's greatest talents to grow. Neutralizing weaknesses requires that you give the employee the help he or she needs to be able to do their job to the required competency level, but not necessarily exceed that level. For example, you don't want to spend an inordinate amount of time focusing on someone's weaknesses. And you certainly don't want to spend an inordinate amount of time pushing someone down a path that he or she is uncomfortable doing or developing a skill set that the person dislikes—even if he or she is capable of accomplishing great results. That's a destructive place to be.

When we focus on the weaknesses of a person, we can actually make the person weaker or even insecure. When we neutralize weaknesses and redirect our energy toward a potential leader's strongest gifts and talents, we have the chance to create superstar performers, confident men and women, and exceptional contributors to the organization overall. The results can be extraordinary.

When you identify and fuel a person's strengths, you better equip him or her for growth and success. Plus you build confidence. And this makes the organization stronger as well. The organization and the future leader come together to create a career plan that works in alignment with the organization's mission and vision as well as the individual's desires and intrinsic motivation. This is the direction this book and its certification program will provide.

The Purpose of Having a Personalized Leader's Development Plan

The purpose of having a leadership development plan (sometimes called an individual development plan), is to grow the talent and employees' strengths throughout your organization. It has little to do with employee retention, or anyone paying you back, or appreciating what you've done for them. That's not the way it works. As Zig Ziglar once said, "If you help enough other people get everything they want in life, you will get everything you want and more." This especially applies to leadership development plans.

If you help an employee plan a career strategy that is enormously successful and he or she chooses to leave your organization, that is their choice and you've done the right thing.

Your intentions toward every future leader should be authentic for their growth and not self-serving. Leadership development planning is a long-lasting and powerful tool. How you manage the responsibility will be up to you. But yes, people will leave and prosper. And in the end, that serves human kind. Everyone wins.

Don't Focus on a Leader Leaving

Few people devote their entire work lives to one organization. Today's managers are well aware that if an employee stays with an organization five or six years, that's a good run. Most Gen Xers and Gen Yers are not going to devote the next 30 years to any one organization like their grandparents did. That's not the way our fluid, faster-than-ever, virtual and hybrid workplace is built.

If you get the best someone has to offer for a few years, then that's about all you can expect. If you get more than that, consider it a bonus—take it and be grateful for the loyalty and dedication that person has put forward. It may just simply be a time for the employee to move on for a wide variety of reasons. The key is in the relationships we build along the way. Accept that as leaders, we all evolve. You'll be glad you did.

Seven-Step Process for Leadership and Personal Employee Development Planning

The process for creating leadership and personal employee development plans can be whatever you want it to be. Experience tells us the collaborative effort in designing a plan makes it stronger and more fluid. As a leader, you can guide the process and help to facilitate the success of the plan by collaborating with the individual on seven easy steps that examine the following key areas:

- Competencies
- Long-Range Goals
- Short-Range Goals
- Strategies

- Action Steps/Timelines
- Resources Toolkit
- Measurable Outcomes

The following process allows for examination of a person's strengths and competencies and their capacity to grow. It sets both short- and long-range goals. It allows for discussion of strategy, provides ongoing resources, and then puts into place measurable outcomes desired by the coach and the aspiring leader.

Competencies	Long-range Goals	Short-range Goals	Strategies

Action Steps/ Timelines	Resources/Toolkits	Measurable Outcomes

Every plan starts with establishing talents and competency. It's not about wishing you had this or that talent. It's about identifying your strengths, not your challenges. List yours in the template here, or make a new template for your future plans. Here are some examples of what a leader or emerging leader might write in the columns.

Competencies	Long-range Goals	Short-range Goals	Strategies
▪ List your soft skills and your technical abilities and skills ▪ This is how my competencies and talents match my career choices ▪ Collaborative sessions and coaching I will need include: __________ ▪ Training I will require to reach my goals: __________ ▪ Research I need to complete ▪ Milestones I'd like to accomplish ▪ My strongest motivation to achieve my best ▪ Here's how I see the big picture	▪ Here's how I see the big picture ▪ Future opportunities I can envision ▪ How I will act the part now ▪ What I must do long-term to achieve my goals ▪ Degrees or certifications I will need to move ahead ▪ Who will coach me? ▪ Who can I count on to mentor me along the way?	▪ Things I can do right now to move forward ▪ What I can do today ▪ What I can do in a week ▪ What I can do in a month ▪ What I can do in one year (Be specific with the above timelines) ▪ What I will do to prepare for the future ▪ This is how much money I will need ▪ How long my professional training will last	▪ Strategies for long- and short-term goals ▪ Who I want on my team ▪ Name the players: __________ __________ ▪ What I will ask each team member to do ▪ How I'll make this development plan an effective strategic tool ▪ Ways I'll establish my vision and mission ▪ How I'll handle change ▪ My can-do attitude will look like this: __________ __________ __________

Action Steps/ Timelines	Resources/ Toolkits	Measurable Outcomes
▪ My list of specific action steps I need to take in order of completion ▪ Agreements or contracts I will need ▪ Review and revise my checklist with a coach ▪ Name my milestones and how I'll address each one ▪ What's working? ▪ What's not working? ▪ What can I eliminate? What can I add?	▪ Things that help me to learn at a higher level ▪ Future technology I will need ▪ People I will seek outside my organization to help me ▪ My list of resources I will need to grow	▪ What have I enjoyed the most about getting to this point? ▪ On a scale of 1 to 5, with 5 being the most advanced, how much have I progressed? ▪ What percentage will I assign to my improvement? 10% improvement? 50%? More? ▪ How will my personal development help grow my organization and improve productivity and performance? ▪ What processes can I help improve? ▪ Here is the feedback I have received on my effectiveness (list comments from others here)

When you take time to develop a plan, you become the architect of your leadership talent and personal growth.

Let's Get Started and Aim for the Stars

Every aspiring leader appreciates a coach or advisor who can help extrapolate and identify their specific goals and dreams. It's a process, which often begins by sitting down with a future leader and helping to identify big-picture goals, dreams, and measurable objectives or outcomes. This is the part where you are shooting for the stars. Think big! Start out by having a relaxed and casual conversation about the employee's unique interests and talents. Inquire about his or her current position and how things are going, ask if the employee is interested in any special assignments, training courses, or ways to contribute to the department he or she works in. This is your time to practice deep listening. A future leader will always share their bigger, greater desires if you take time to ask and listen first.

Inquire about the future leader's goals. Show your concern about family, using sensitivity and inquiring about community interests. These are things that can greatly impact leadership development planning. For example, a great position might be available at another location in your organization. For example, it may be timely to ask the person whether he or she would consider relocating to a different city or state. If the answer is yes, this could become a goal within the plan. If the answer is no, then the plan will take a different direction and reflect those choices. In addition, the worker might share with you that right now would be a difficult time to move elsewhere, but in two years the timing would be better. Then you could add *relocating for a new position* into the long-range goal category of this person's plan instead of the short-range category.

Offer resources you know of that are available both inside and outside the organization. Consult other departments for assistance in identifying additional resources or tools. Something to beware of: sometimes a leader uses their own career development as a reference point for guiding the development of others. This can be a mistake. We can all easily fall into this trap without ever thinking about it. But what worked for you as a manager or supervisor in years past might not be the best plan for today's technologically advanced and faster speed worker who is sitting across from you now. **Be relative. Be current. Be in the now.**

Here's where you start the preparations of a customized leadership development plan. Set up specific dates and times to meet with the worker to assess progress and changes and help him or her revise the plan as you go along. The plan will grow with time. Provide assessment resources so the employee can establish a baseline of competency and self-score himself or herself in areas in which he or she can grow and flourish.

Don't rely on an annual review timeframe to go over this plan. This is a work in progress. It will require ongoing lengthier meetings to breathe life into the document.

This is a time when growing talent and a wide variety of development issues can be unique and potentially exhausting. Yes, the challenges are there, but the rewards are great. How you equip yourself to develop leadership—like using this book as your guide, for example—

will separate you from the rest and move potential leaders in your organization in a positive direction.

Remember that exceptional leadership development plans, the ones that make the greatest difference, always rely on moving forward and taking action. This book was written to provide you with both and for experiencing successful outcomes.

CONCLUSION

Dear Leader,

I want to thank you for embarking on this journey with me. Being a leader is accepting the great responsibility to make things happen to improve and shape the world for the better. Leadership may begin with you, but it ends with others. It has the potential to be a valuable and lifelong endeavor toward not only your personal growth and success, but for those around you as well. Good leaders encourage others, nurture the growth of those around them, see the potential in what's to come, and grow their capacity to initiate these changes. It is our job as leaders to bring out the best in others so they can achieve the success of their dreams. And when you begin to affect your follower's followers, that is when you know you are on the right path.

At the beginning of this book, I explained that you are on a journey toward a vision of who you want to become as a leader. I hope you have discovered as you have read this book that being a leader is so much more than achieving your own personal vision or wielding power. Leaders build relationships, grow capacities, have vision, and empower others to lead. Many people with the potential to become leaders do not believe they have what it takes, but leadership is a learned skill. Even if it is out of your comfort zone to interact with people, it is a skill you can learn. If you do not have the needed qualities, you can develop them.

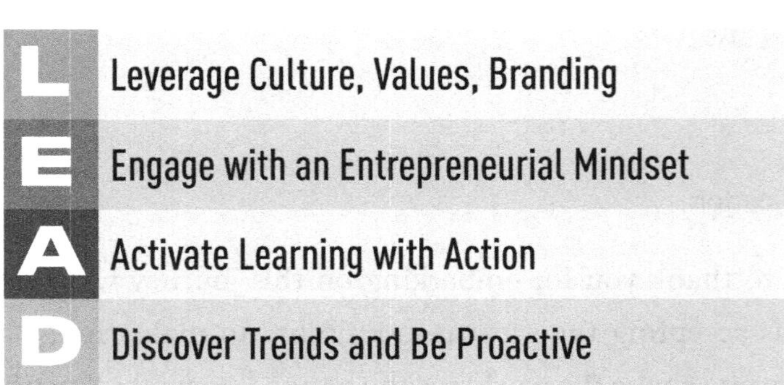

Leadership goes far beyond a title and having nice things. In fact, it is not about your power at all. It is about building relationships. It is a state of being, an attitude of mind, an atmosphere of growth for others as well as yourself. Leaders do not leave the world neutral—they always have an impact either for the better or worse—so be sure to do better once you know better. Own your mistakes and learn from them. Be humble and use your core values to guide good decision making toward your end goals. Coach others to dig deep and find within themselves their best attributes, then encourage them to use those strengths and skills to bring about change in those who follow them.

The world needs good leaders like you, ones who can envision beyond the here and now—to see people, places, and things not as they are today, but as they could be. That is at the heart of leadership. Great leaders follow their core values and the principles that govern ethical behavior. Principles have power, and when you use them to guide you to help others succeed, the goodness multiplies. The decisions that leaders make have the capacity to affect the lives of people, families, schools, communities, organizations, governments, and even entire nations.

It all starts by taking the first step. I invite you to take this vow of personal responsibility with me.

Dear Leader: Vow of Personal Responsibility[5]

- I vow to be responsible for my life experience.
- I am responsible for how I use time.
- I am responsible for how I use money.
- I am responsible for the status of my relationships.
- I am responsible for getting my needs met.
- I am the creator of my experiences.

Even though I may not see my choices immediately in challenging circumstances or situations, I am willing to recognize the fact that choices are always available to me.

The more I recognize my choices, the more responsible I become. The less I complain, judge, and blame others, the more empowered I become.

I am not a victim to my emotions or to the situation around me, or to other people's behaviors.

I agree to recognize that when I have an unwanted experience, and as a result fall into patterns of blame, resentment, justification, or judgment, it is possibly because I failed to ask for what I want. Or perhaps I failed to set a boundary, failed to speak up, or I was unrealistic in my expectations, or in some other way unclear in my communication.

---

5 Published with permission of Marlene Chism, bestselling author of *Conflict to Courage: How to Stop Avoiding and Start Leading* (Berrett-Koelher, 2022)

I accept that even in my disappointments there is an opportunity to grow, to learn how to communicate more effectively, to step into a new truth, and to see others differently.

I reap the rewards and the consequences of the choices I make, as well as the unconscious reactions I have.

Because I have choice, I am responsible, and because I am responsible, I am empowered.

I gladly accept the role of creator and take the vow of responsibility in all areas of my life personally and professionally.

Signed ____

Date____

So dear leader, I will leave you with this message: Your growth does not stop today. I encourage you to keep learning, keep doing, keep striving to make good decisions for the benefit of the greater good. This leadership movement we are part of has the power to make big and positive changes in the lives of those around us, and the future we make for our children's children. Join me as I continue to inspire and encourage leaders just like you, because together we form a choir whose voices are strong and united and far-reaching. We sing louder together than alone.

APPENDIX I:

Quick Reference Learning Labs for Sticky Situations

This book is a comprehensive leadership field guide built to help prepare you for unexpected encounters that may take you by surprise. We all can use a quick grab-and-go tool to get us through a sticky situation and back on track with clear and healthy communications. This appendix gives you sample scenarios you can use to prepare yourself ahead of time so you can handle real-life scenarios in the moment.

These are what I refer to as Learning Labs—brief troubleshooting scenarios and corresponding solutions—that encapsulate everyday sticky situations where you may be called on to address issues at hand. Each lab refers briefly to a possible challenge you may encounter, the desired outcome, any trigger points you may come across, tools you can use, and a possible direction you may choose to take going forward. When you encounter a situation similar to what's in the learning lab, you can use these tools to work toward a solution.

These are not meant to be narratives of workplace scenarios or skills. They are easy-to-reference, grab-and-go, bite-sized chunks of information you can apply, adapt, and modify to your own needs as a leader—no matter what your level of leadership abilities.

Learning Lab #1: Active Listening

DISCUSSION STRATEGIES

Learning Tool

- Comprehend – Retain – Respond
- External and Internal Factors to Consider When Actively Listening

Desired Outcomes: What changes in behavior do you expect?

1. Remove environmental barriers (quiet area)
2. Have right attitude and be open to listening
3. Good body language (eye contact, posture)
4. Empathize
5. Take notes
6. Be receptive and open-minded
7. Summarize key points
8. Do not interrupt
9. Keep emotions under control
10. Don't be quick to respond
11. Don't judge
12. Put speaker at ease
13. Don't antagonize
14. Use expansion statements: "Tell me more"
15. Be attentive to tone and volume
16. Be patient
17. Have no distractions
18. Listen more than speak
19. Don't assume
20. Ask questions
21. Respond to what is being said, not the person
22. Be engaged with mental and physical focus

IDENTIFY NEGATIVE TRIGGERS

Learning Tool

- Words or Non-Verbal Behavior That Produce Negative Reactions
- How problems occur: Triggers — Escalation — Crisis — Recovery

What behaviors, patterns, or words cause negative actions?

1. Communication destroyers: Anger warning signs — Negative feedback (harsh criticism and temper) Body language
2. Making assumptions, bad attitude, not thinking before you speak
3. Lack of objectivity, sensitivity, or empathy

IDENTIFY CHANGE MOTIVATORS

Learning Tool

- Self-Motivation: Develop Confidence — Focus — Direction
- Self-Respect: It starts with leadership
- 3 Most Powerful Motivators:
    1. Fear
    2. Incentives
    3. Personal Growth and Development

What would motivate me to want to see change in active listening skills?

1. Turning disconnection into sharing: Opinions — Suggestions — Ideas — Collaboration
2. Having consequences to non-compliance
3. Eliminating stress with best practices
4. Increasing individual and team pride
5. Celebrating measurable success
6. Building a better working environment

IDENTIFY SOLUTIONS

Learning Tool

- Method or Process of Solving Problems
- Win-Win Solutions

What can I do to improve active listening skills?

1. Demonstrate positive behavior
2. Ask open-ended questions
3. Design personal action plan to improve performance
4. Participate in effective meeting dialog
5. Be fearless in sharing differences of opinion appropriately
6. Actively participate in continuous learning opportunities
7. Brainstorm to find more creative solutions

IDENTIFY OBSTACLES

Learning Tool

- Something that prevents progress

What obstacles might I encounter when trying to improve the art of active listening?

1. Handling stress
2. Personal ego and denial that problems exist
3. Using only tested solutions instead of creating new ones

DASHBOARD METRICS

- Improvement Requires Positive Change
- Change Is Contingent Upon Interdependence and Influencing, or Persuading Others

What measurements will demonstrate that outcomes have been reached?

1. How many instructional misunderstandings have occurred? At what cost?
2. How many action plans have been written or not written correctly where listening was a concern?
3. Are people asking more questions for clarification?
4. How many more "coaching-in-the-moment" sessions are you conducting?
5. Do you "correct and redirect" negative behaviors on the spot?

Learning Lab #2: Self-Improvement

DISCUSSION STRATEGIES

Learning Tool

- Making the Best Choices to Achieve the Best Outcomes by Optimizing Performance and Maximizing Relationships

Desired Outcomes: What changes in behavior do you expect?

1. Reduce stress
2. Manage emotions
3. Resolve conflicts
4. Deal with challenges
5. Connect through non-verbal communication
6. Respect others
7. Have a healthy work and personal life balance

IDENTIFY NEGATIVE TRIGGERS

Learning Tool

- Words or Non-Verbal Behavior That Produce Negative Reactions
- How Problems Occur: Triggers — Escalation — Crisis — Recovery

What behaviors, patterns, or words cause negative actions?

1. Bringing personal stress into the workplace
2. Negative self-image and self-confidence
3. Lack of training and skill

IDENTIFY CHANGE MOTIVATORS

Learning Tool

- Self-Motivation: Develop Confidence — Focus — Direction
- 3 Most Powerful Motivators
  1. Fear
  2. Incentives
  3. Personal Growth and Development

What would motivate me to seek continued self-improvement?

1. Advancement opportunities
2. Job security
3. Career change options
4. Improved relationships
5. Improved self-image
6. Respect from others

IDENTIFY SOLUTIONS

Learning Tool

- Method or Process of Solving Problems
- Win-Win Solutions

As a leader what can I do to improve a team member's self-image?

1. Praise positive performance
2. Provide training for self-improvement
3. Mentor employees for advancement opportunities
4. Provide stress-busting activities
5. Manage environmental comforts

IDENTIFY OBSTACLES

Learning Tool

- Something That Prevents Progress

As a leader, what obstacles might I encounter when trying to help my team move forward in challenging times?

1. Being in denial of needing self-improvement (either by thinking you are perfect, or not good enough to advance)
2. No drive, passion, or motivation (working 9 to 5 and collecting a paycheck attitude)
3. No career path within the company
4. Supervisor intimidation for fear of job replacement

PRACTICING LEARNING SKILLS

1. How do you balance work and personal life right now?
2. Where do you want to be professionally in one, two, or three years from now? How are you preparing?

DASHBOARD METRICS

- Improvement Requires Positive Change
- Change Is Contingent Upon Interdependence and Influencing, or Persuading Others

What measurements will demonstrate that outcomes have been reached?

1. Have stress levels decreased?
2. Have peer-peer and manager-team relationships improved?
3. What positive changes have occurred?
4. Have teams been more open to take on new challenges?

Learning Lab #3: Difficult or Unprofessional Behavior

DISCUSSION STRATEGIES

Learning Tool

- Professional Growth Is Based on Behaviors, Not Opinions

Desired Outcomes: What changes in behavior do you expect?

1. Keeping your cool when you want to argue
2. Being open to different opinions instead of acting domineering
3. Sticking with facts and not exaggerating or lying
4. Respecting company policies
5. Finding ways to deal with personal issues that enhance the working environment and relationships

IDENTIFY NEGATIVE TRIGGERS

Learning Tool

- Words or Non-Verbal Behavior That Produce Negative Reactions
- How Problems Occur: Triggers — Escalation — Crisis — Recovery

What behavior patterns cause negative actions?

1. Inappropriate outbursts
2. Not respecting other's time
3. Not taking responsibility
4. Bringing drama to work
5. Not attempting to resolve problems
6. Continuous conflicts with co-workers
7. Poor attitude

IDENTIFY CHANGE MOTIVATORS

Learning Tool

- Self-Motivation: Develop Confidence — Focus — Direction
- Motivation Factors:
  1. Satisfaction for Good Results
  2. Failure as a Learning Experience
  3. Recognition for Applying Techniques
  4. Consequences for Negative Behaviors/Poor Results

What would motivate me to eliminate unprofessional or poor behavior?

1. A more pleasant work environment
2. Low employee energy
3. Negative actions
4. Not feeling proud of the organization's culture
5. Stagnant job opportunities
6. Loss of co-worker's respect and support

IDENTIFY SOLUTIONS

Learning Tool

- Method or Process of Solving Problems
- Win-Win Solutions and Problem Solving

As a leader what can I do to eliminate energy-draining behavior?

1. Coaching and mentoring programs
2. Communicating better processes
3. Recognizing small successes — Offering ongoing feedback
4. Using company policies as an honorable commitment to being our best

IDENTIFY OBSTACLES

Learning Tool

- Something That Prevents Progress

As a leader what obstacles will I encounter when trying to eliminate poor behavior?

1. Dealing with situations that cross over into human resources and legal concerns
2. Accommodating for temporary stress situations: death – illness – divorce – mental health

PRACTICING LEARNING SKILLS AND ROLE PLAY

1. Leader is investigating a conflict between co-workers that may have led to verbal abuse
2. Leader explains the drawbacks of unprofessional behavior and the impact on the organization and its people

DASHBOARD METRICS

- Improvement Requires Positive Change
- Change Is Contingent on Positive Influences and Persuading Others

What measurements demonstrate positive outcomes have been reached?

1. Profitability
2. Increase in overall performance
3. Lower customer complaints—Higher customer satisfaction
4. Happier employees

Learning Lab #4: Integrity

DISCUSSION STRATEGIES

Learning Tool

- **Ethics**
- **Values**
- **Influencers**

Desired Outcomes: What changes in behavior do you expect?

1. Golden Rule philosophy upheld
2. Honesty as the foundation of good communication and relationships
3. Confidentiality
4. Leading by example sets the tone for ethical and influential behavior
5. Integrity as a required characteristic

IDENTIFY NEGATIVE TRIGGERS

Learning Tool

- Words or Non-Verbal Behavior That Produce Negative Reactions
- How Problems Occur: Triggers — Escalation — Crisis — Recovery

What behavior patterns are associated with a lack of integrity?

1. Unfair treatment of individuals
2. Environment of fear
3. Retribution for ideas and opinions
4. Dishonest role models
5. Lack of diversity or prejudice
6. Bad mouthing others
7. Lack of trustworthiness

IDENTIFY CHANGE MOTIVATORS

Learning Tool

- Self-Motivation: Develop Confidence — Focus — Direction
- Motivation: Pride in a job well done — Pride in co-workers — Pride in the company culture — Trust in leadership

What would motivate me to inspire integrity in the workplace?

1. Instilling an environment of motivation, pride, and long-term success
2. Growing people to become better leaders to secure higher level positions (dream job) and ultimate succession
3. Enhance company reputation for leadership
4. Be a noble role model
5. Be perceived as a fair and equitable leader

IDENTIFY SOLUTIONS

Learning Tool

- Method or Process of Solving Problems
- Win-Win Solutions

As a respected leader, what can I do to lead my team with integrity?

1. Provide leadership training at all levels
2. Monitor integrity benchmarks: Vision and Goals — Leadership — Trust — Culture
3. Develop system for handling unethical behavior
4. Demonstrate integrity in your own daily actions
5. Subscribe to a code of impressive conduct—Instill that everyone is an ambassador
6. Ensure that the workplace has effective systems to manage ethical and security risks
7. Foster continuous learning, personal growth, and improvement

IDENTIFY OBSTACLES

Learning Tool

- Something that prevents progress

As a leader, what obstacles might I encounter when trying to inspire integrity?

1. Insecure team members who crave control, recognition, or credit without merit
2. Learn from errors of judgment
3. Watch for "short-cuts" or easy ways to success

PRACTICING LEARNING SKILLS AND ROLE PLAY

1. How is your organization better because you are in it? Why?
2 Are you a better person because you are a part of this organization? Explain.
3. Share an "integrity moment" in which you or your team have participated

DASHBOARD METRICS

- Improvement Requires Positive Change
- Change Is Contingent Upon Interdependence and Influencing, or Persuading Others

What measurements will demonstrate that outcomes have been reached?

1. What does integrity look like in your organization?
2. What stories of great integrity do your share with others?
3. Are people doing the right thing because it's the right thing to do, or because they are required to or forced to do so?

Learning Lab #5: Gossip

Discussion Strategies

Learning Tool

- Impact on Coworkers — Leadership – Overall Organization

Desired Outcomes: What changes in behavior do you expect?

1. Minimize disruptions in workflow
2. Protect employees' feelings
3. Repair damaged relationships
4. Increase morale
5. Inspire motivation and collaboration

IDENTIFY NEGATIVE TRIGGERS

Learning Tool

- Words or Non-Verbal Behavior That Produce Negative Reactions
- How Problems Occur: Triggers — Escalation — Crisis — Recovery

What behavior patterns cause negative actions?

1. Person not at work on a given day becomes target for gossip
2. Employees siding against each other or outside of work
3. Sudden dismissal of employee and its reaction
4. Unpopular promotion of an individual
5. Someone intimidated by new employee
6. Suspicions of management relationships or unpopular decisions
7. Employee who is praised in public too often or seen as a favorite

IDENTIFY CHANGE MOTIVATORS

Learning Tool

- Self-Motivation: Develop Confidence — Focus — Direction
- Motivation: To Become a Better Communicator — Long-term Career Opportunities

What would motivate a leader to stop the gossip?

1. Greater productivity
2. Preventing litigious situations
3. Enjoy coming to work
4. Preserving positive company reputation
5. Creating high-spirited teams and teamwork
6. Trust

IDENTIFY SOLUTIONS

Learning Tool

- Method or Process of Solving Problems
- Win-Win Solutions

As a leader what can I do to eliminate gossip?

1. Address gossip at the start
2. Set boundaries and expectations
3. As a leader, do not initiate or participate in the gossip circle

IDENTIFY OBSTACLES

Learning Tool

- Something That Prevents Progress

As a leader what obstacles might be encountered trying to eliminate gossip?

1. You could become the subject of new gossip. How would you deal with that reality?
2. Offenders could escalate to more difficult behaviors if they feel sought after
3. Retaliation may result

PRACTICING LEARNING SKILLS AND ROLE PLAY

- Team members create examples of workplace gossip and ways it can be stopped or discouraged by others

DASHBOARD METRICS

- Improvement Requires Positive Change
- Change Requires Positive Influencers

What measurements will demonstrate that outcomes have been reached?

1. Have you heard less gossip lately?
2. How do new hires feel about their new peer relationships?
3. What changes have you made in your communication to set a better example?
4. Include tips and tools on how to handle gossiping employees in your communications training

Learning Lab #6: Negativity

DISCUSSION STRATEGIES

Learning Tool

- Insecurity — Lack of Confidence — Control
- Zaps Energy

Desired Outcomes: What changes in behavior do you expect?

1. Focus on self-esteem issues
2. Observe and listen for deliberate misinformation
3. Correct and redirect in the moment
4. Catch people doing things right—don't look for fault unless it appears

IDENTIFY NEGATIVE TRIGGERS

Learning Tool

- Words or Non-Verbal Behavior That Produce Negative Reactions
- How Problems Occur: Triggers — Escalation — Crisis — Recovery

What behavior may cause negative actions?

1. Start by eliminating root causes of negativity: unrealistic workloads — mismanagement — anxiety about the future — lack of personal and professional goals — lack of deserved recognition from leadership

IDENTIFY CHANGE MOTIVATORS

Learning Tool

- Self-Motivation: Develop Confidence — Focus — Direction
- Motivation: Raise Morale — Build Confidence — Change Energy in the Environment — Focus on the Good

What motivates a leader to eliminate negativity?

1. Having a high-morale working environment
2. Energy can be redirected to reach goals and reward people
3. Negativity drains energy exponentially—positivity raises energy exponentially and creates opportunity

IDENTIFY SOLUTIONS

Learning Tool

- Method or Process of Solving Problems
- Win-Win Solutions

As a leader, what can I do to eliminate negativity?

1. Provide honest, helpful feedback about negative situations
2. Listen via group discussion — town hall meetings — team lunches
3. Challenge negative thinking with a positive outlook
4. Ask more open-ended questions
5. Perform exit interviews with a positive outlook
6. Recognize the impact of policy and procedure changes that greatly affect employees personally: work hours — pay — benefits — overtime — dress code — office relocation — working conditions — job requirements
7. Discuss and explain any major change transitions for full comprehension
8. Don't ignore negativity. By doing so you may be giving permission for it to continue
9. Counsel complainers and get to the root cause of their opinions

IDENTIFY OBSTACLES

Learning Tool

- Something That Prevents Progress

As a leader, what obstacles could you encounter trying to eliminate negativity?

1. Someone is upset because they were not promoted
2. Another leader's negative attitude
3. Unconsciously encouraging negativity by body language, tone, or voicing opinions about company policy changes, or leadership decisions
4. Poor productivity
5. Negativity can be brought on by a person with a bad attitude, or by getting news you don't like, or being involved in a negative situation. Be aware it won't automatically just go away.

PRACTICING LEARNING SKILLS AND ROLE PLAY

1. Ask an employee what they believe others think about their approach or attitude? Is that person aware?
2. In a role play, ask "What would you do?" "How would you handle the situation?" "What steps would you take?" etc.

DASHBOARD METRICS

- Improvement Requires Positive Change
- Change Is Contingent Upon Interdependence and Influencing, or Persuading Others

What measurements will demonstrate that leadership goals have been reached?

1. What positive steps have negative influencers made? Who's resisting? Why?
2. What changes have you as a leader made to offset negativity?
3. What's the most negative issue today that generates the most complaints or concerns?
4. How can this be solved from the inside out?

Learning Lab #7: Handling Sabotaging Co-Workers

DISCUSSION STRATEGIES

Learning Tool

- Ways to Handle Deliberate Damage, Interference, or Disruption That Reduces Productivity and Harms the Organization

Desired Outcomes: What changes in behavior do you expect?

1. Stop the "blame game"
2. Stop manipulation
3. Don't let saboteurs anger or frustrate the team
4. Invoke humor to diffuse tension
5. When addressing the situation, do it with logic, not emotion

IDENTIFY NEGATIVE TRIGGERS

Learning Tool

- Words or Non-Verbal Behavior That Produce Negative Reactions
- How Problems Occur: Triggers – Escalation – Crisis – Recovery

What sabotages the team?

1. People who spread rumors and aim to destroy reputations
2. People who take credit for your work
3. People who fail to do their work as part of a team project
4. People who give you impossible assignments
5. People who give you more work than than they give to other co-workers
6. People who blame others when things go wrong but never take responsibility
7. People who regularly make demeaning remarks and put-downs
8. People who undermine, or fire, capable workers because they feel threatened

IDENTIFY CHANGE MOTIVATORS

Learning Tool

- Self-Motivation: Develop Confidence — Focus — Direction
- Motivation: Positive Leadership and Accountability

Why be concerned with saboteurs?

1. Personal and professional damage
2. Manipulative behavior can do long-term damage to the organization and teams

IDENTIFY SOLUTIONS

Learning Tool

- Method or Process of Solving Problems
- Win-Win Solutions

As a leader, what can I do to put a halt to someone who intentionally sabotages the team?

1. Understand different personality types and mentor appropriately
2. Do your best to influence a positive behavior change first, whenever possible
3. Document the actions of sabotaging behavior
4. Watch for new employees to be the target of saboteurs
5. Never make it personal
6. Use company policy to initiate performance action plans and termination procedures

IDENTIFY OBSTACLES

Learning Tool

- Something that Prevents Progress

As a leader, what obstacles can I expect from a person who sabotages others?

1. Shining stars will slowly leave the organization because of sabotaging environments
2. Watch for subtle saboteur actions: missing information — mysterious destruction of property — missing supplies—falsifying information
3. Watch for sudden disengagement (If I'm quiet no one will suspect me)

PRACTICING LEARNING SKILLS AND ROLE PLAY

1. Audit worker's performance without notice
2. Ask employees to share a story of their experience and how they handled it

DASHBOARD METRICS

- Improvement Requires Positive Change
- Change Is Contingent Upon Interdependence and Influencing, or Persuading Others

What measures will demonstrate your success?

1. Ask a saboteur to account for his or her destructive behavior
2. Have you received any complaints from employees who fear a saboteur? Get names. Remain confidential.
3. Ask employees how they are being treated by their peers — watch for body language

Learning Lab #8: Office Politics

DISCUSSION STRATEGIES

Learning Tool

- Office Politics Definition: Objective Is to Gain Advantage by Manipulation and Game Playing
- Differences About People at Work (Opinions and Conflicts of Interest)

Desired Outcomes: What changes in behavior do you expect?

1. Making better choices when reacting to people and situations
2. Keeping the focus on business objectives and not getting personal
3. Having focus on how to influence positively
4. Seeking to better understand
5. Creative ways both parties can win

IDENTIFY NEGATIVE TRIGGERS

Learning Tool

- Words or Non-Verbal Behavior That Produce Negative Reactions
- How Problems Occur: Triggers — Escalation — Crisis — Recovery

What behaviors cause negative actions?

1. People unreasonably seeking a promotion
2. People who want their ideas chosen above others
3. People who want to be in the limelight without hard work
4. Lack of supervision and control in the workplace
5. Arrogant leaders and managers
6. Jealous colleagues
7. People who aspire something beyond their control in a short period of time

IDENTIFY CHANGE MOTIVATORS

Learning Tool

- Self-Motivation: Develop Confidence — Focus — Direction
- Motivation: Fairness, Equitable Working Conditions

What would motivate me to correct and redirect office politics?

1. Spending more time on job responsibilities than personally motivated issues
2. Having balance of positive self-interest and group respect
3. Remove primary negative influencers

IDENTIFY SOLUTIONS

Learning Tool

- Method or Process of Solving Problems
- Win-Win Solutions

As a leader, what can I do to eliminate office politics?

1. Recognize and reward employee contributions
2. Assist co-workers to build quality relationships
3. Seek upper-level mentors for guidance
4. Help employees understand each other
5. Disrespect will not be tolerated
6. Provide soft-skills training and coaching for collaboration
7. Discourage cliques

18. Make decisions using logic and common sense procedures, not succumbing to pressure from favored players

IDENTIFY OBSTACLES

Learning Tool

- Something That Prevents Progress

As a leader, what obstacles might I encounter when trying to control office politics?

1. Rumors can cause perceptual problems
2. Being kept out of the loop or being ostracized
3. Power and influencers will not go away — It's how you maintain your integrity around it

PRACTICING LEARNING SKILLS AND ROLE PLAY

1. Have discussion on: Is it better to play or pass on office politics?
2. Have you ever been a victim of office politics? How did that affect your career?

DASHBOARD METRICS

- Improvement Requires Positive Change
- Change Is Contingent Upon Interdependence and Influencing, or Persuading Others

What types of measures will demonstrate that outcomes have been reached?

1. On a scale of 1–10, how pervasive are your office politics?
2. At what level are office politics most problematic?
3. What win-win strategies have you initiated to decrease office political behavior?

Learning Lab #9: Trust

DISCUSSION STRATEGIES

Learning Tool

- Belief in Trust — Trusting Everyone Will Do Their Part —
- Belief in Trust as Mutual versus Self-Serving
- Enhance Culture of Trust by Creating Environmental Conditions of Open Communication
- Being Accountable — Being Honest
- Results of Trustworthiness: Credibility — Integrity
- Reliability — Commitment — Long-term Relationships

Desired Outcomes: What changes in behavior do you expect when trust is built?

1. Improved communications
2. Improved relationships
3. Mistakes become learning experiences
4. Creating trust by: Building self-esteem — Supporting and praise for colleagues — Constructive and ongoing feedback — Respect for confidentiality — Standing up for each other — Team spirit — Avoiding gossip and criticism— Appreciating people and their differences
5. Being sensitive to the areas that directly impact the level of trust people have in the organization: Vision — Values — Compensation — Work Environment — HR Decisions

IDENTIFY NEGATIVE TRIGGERS

Learning Tool

- Words or Non-Verbal Behavior That Produce Negative Reactions
- How Problems Occur: Triggers — Escalation — Crisis — Recovery

What behaviors cause negative actions?

1. Actions That Destroy Trust
    - Deception: Failure to Tell the Truth
    - Lies of Omission
    - Failure to Demonstrate Expectations (Walk the Talk)
    - Failure to Deliver What You Say You Will Do
    - Making Changes for No Reason (Mood — Deadlines)
2. Inconsistent behaviors
3. Always seeking personal versus shared gains
4. Unwillingness to consider other points of view
5. Warning signs that trust is an issue: active, inaccurate grapevine — Low Initiative — High Turnover — High Fear — Turf Wars — Defensiveness

IDENTIFY CHANGE MOTIVATORS

Learning Tool

- Self-Motivation: Develop Confidence — Focus — Direction
- Motivation: Good and bad lessons learned — Respect

What would motivate me to create a more trusting workplace?

1. Eliminate suspicions of others
2. Employees working from home
3. Ongoing virtual assignments
4. Dependable performance from a distance with less supervision

IDENTIFY SOLUTIONS

Learning Tool

- Method or Process of Solving Problems
- Win-Win Solutions

As a leader, what can I do to enhance trust?

1. Creating trust is an intentional and deliberate process involving planning and implementation
2. You must be competent to produce results by gaining credibility and trust
3. Adhere to diverse, forward-thinking, inventive business standards
4. Set an example by being accountable
5. Ask people at meetings to share experiences and work-related lessons
6. Ask employees to assist in creating innovative solutions
7. Use "us" and "we" instead of "I" and "me"

IDENTIFY OBSTACLES

Learning Tool

- Something That Prevents Progress

As a leader, what obstacles will I possibly encounter when trying to build trust?

1. Feeling betrayed by colleagues
2. Passive-aggressive resistance

PRACTICING LEARNING SKILLS AND ROLE PLAY

- Create your own meaning for the letters in the word T R U S T
- Failing to tell the truth about a workplace situation

DASHBOARD METRICS

- Improvement Requires Positive Change
- Change Is Contingent and Includes Influence

What types of measures will demonstrate that outcomes have been reached?

1. How many incidences of conflict have occurred?
2. What are the top 3 issues regarding trust that you spend most of your time correcting?

Learning Lab #10: Respect

DISCUSSION STRATEGIES

Learning Tool

- RESPECT Acronym
  R = Reputation
  E = Ethics
  S = Sense
  P = Perception
  E = Effort
  C = Civility
  T = Time and Place
- Consideration for Self and Others

Desired Outcomes: What changes in behavior do you expect?

1. Respect for opinions and increased engagement
2. Respectful attitudes for decreased stress
3. Respect and appreciation for diversity and differences for an inclusive environment
4. Respect for courteous behavior
5. Respect for empowering learning and advancement
6. Respect for others' time
7. Respect for the sake of respect

IDENTIFY NEGATIVE TRIGGERS

Learning Tool

- Words or Non-Verbal Behavior That Produce Negative Reactions
- How Problems Occur: Triggers — Escalation — Crisis — Recovery

What behavior-pattern-words cause negative actions?

1. People who won't listen to the opinion of others
2. People who bring up multiple negative issues at once
3. People who believe there is only one answer and it is theirs
4. People who try to force you to agree
5. People who don't apologize for being offensive
6. People who can't admit they made a mistake
7. People who can't move on past conflict

IDENTIFY CHANGE MOTIVATORS

Learning Tool

- Self-Motivation: Develop Confidence — Focus — Direction
- Motivation: Desirability of Respect and Kindness

What would motivate me to instill respect in the workplace?

1. Mutual respect is a core desire
2. Disrespect brings people down
3. Lack of respect wastes precious time and energy
4. Disrespect reduces quality of group decision making

IDENTIFY SOLUTIONS

Learning Tool

- Method or Process of Solving Problems
- Win-Win Solutions

As a leader, what can I do to increase respect among my team?

1. Identify disrespect and maintain a non-threatening environment
2. Take quick action to resolve the behavior
3. Allow consequences for repeated disrespectful engagement
4. Give positive feedback to employees who have temporary setbacks

IDENTIFY OBSTACLES

Learning Tool

- Something That Prevents Progress

As a leader, what obstacles might get in my way of building respect?

1. When disrespect becomes rudeness, embarrassment, belittling, and shameful
2. When disrespect becomes bullying
3. When disrespect affects work performance and productivity

PRACTICING LEARNING SKILLS

1. Name all your reactions to seeing someone disrespect someone else

DASHBOARD METRICS

- Change Is Contingent Upon Interdependence and Influencing, or Persuading Others

What types of measures will demonstrate that outcomes have been reached?

1. Have you seen patterns of improvement in response to expected outcomes?
2. What are the most prevalent occurrences of disrespect you've witnessed?

APPENDIX II:

Experiential Applications and Evaluations

One of your keys to success will be the experiential application and feedback you get from using lessons in this book in the real world. Until you apply what you have learned in the environment in which you are working or hope to work, lessons fall short. In the closing part of this book, I am providing you with a special experiential follow-up assignment.

This on-the-job exercise will help measure your effectiveness and skills you have learned reading this book. Please reply to the following:

What specific lessons in this book have you practiced on the job and what were the results and feedback from others?

____

____

____

____

____

____

____

Describe one or more situations you have been able to handle more effectively as a result of reading *Dear Leader*. What was your biggest challenge? How did you apply what you've learned and what were the outcomes?

____

____

____

____

____

____

What tips or tools in this book do you find yourself referring to most frequently?

____

____

____

____

____

____

Add your additional thoughts and comments here:

____

____

____

____

____

____

Make a promise to do an experiential exercise within the next month. Sign and date below.

Signed ____

Date____

> **"IT'S ONLY WHEN WE APPLY WHAT WE LEARN THAT WE CAN LEAD WITH CONFIDENCE AND PERSONAL CONVICTION. IDEAS ARE CRITICAL, BUT PUTTING THOSE IDEAS INTO ACTION IS ESSENTIAL."**
>
> —Dr. Sam Adeyemi

GRATITUDES

Dear Leader is not just a book; it represents a big shift in the building of a leadership movement with the vision to raise high-impact leaders in families, organizations, and nations. It has been my experience that when one is ready for such a shift, providence brings across one's path people that would be helpful for making the shift.

The first person in this instance is Anne Bruce, a Speaker and Author Coach, who brought to bear the full weight of her talents, skills, and experience. She grasped the vision for the shift, being the author of more than 25 books that have been translated into many languages, and having spoken at conferences globally. This book is one part of the vision. Thank you, Anne, for providing incredible leadership for highly skilled members of the editorial and production team. I thank Ben Allen for introducing Anne to me.

I would like to give special thanks to Phyllis Jask, the Editorial Director, for being creative in getting the right structure and feel for the book. Thank you for giving great attention to details and for showing such a high level of commitment, squeezing time out for meetings even when it was difficult.

I thank Brenda Hawkes, the Art Director, for creating an amazing layout for this book. I also thank Philip Studdard and Flip Design Studio, Inc. for the beautiful cover design, and for the quick turnaround time for your work. Thank you, Herbert Kuper and Advanced Photo & Imaging, for taking great shots for my cover photos.

Many amazing people have influenced my leadership journey whom I would love to list individually here, but for space I gratefully thank my family and in-laws (nuclear and extended), mentors, friends, and the amazing staffs, leaders, members, consultants, and volunteers at Success Power, Daystar, and Sam Adeyemi organizations. I also thank the millions who follow me on social media or who have attended my presentations live, online, and on TV. You have been amazing. I am deeply grateful for your love and for believing that we can make the world better by being better leaders.

I'll like to thank our children, Sophie, David, and Adora, not only for serving as sounding boards for the writing and marketing of this book, but for being a vital part of my leadership journey. As we worked on the chapter on Leadership in the Multi-Generational Workplace, I thought of you and felt very proud of the sound values you have inculcated. I have hope that yours and the generations after yours will make our world better.

I want to specially thank my sweetheart, Adenike. Thank you for your understanding, patience, and support, while I pursued this project, just as you've always done. Thank you for teaming with me and complementing me with your amazing personality and bouquet of talents and skills to influence our world for good. I love you.

I have been incredibly favored in my journey. I am very grateful to God for His love, guidance, and help, which have been evident every step of the way in the writing and production of this book. I am truly grateful.

ABOUT THE AUTHOR

Dr. Sam Adeyemi is a global conference speaker and strategic leadership coach, who shifts mindsets so his audiences and clients can see possibilities and become those possibilities. With more than one million followers on social media, Sam is building a movement of high-impact leaders who are shaping the fortunes and destinies of their families, organizations, and nations. He is the bestselling author of the highly acclaimed book *Dear Leader—Your Flagship Guide to Successful Leadership*. He created his High-Impact Leadership Certification Program based on an evidence-based professional survey his team conducted over months on a global scale. The results of that survey are part of the research that has gone into this real-life training and certification program and into his popular leadership book and keynote speeches.

Sam has addressed audiences at the Global Leadership Summit, the Horasis Global Meeting, and other high-impact conferences around the world. He founded Success Power in 1995, which has inspired millions of people through radio, television, and social media to leverage the universal laws of success to improve their lives despite adversity.

Dr. Adeyemi has spoken to over 400,000 leaders in more than 100 countries. His Daystar Leadership Academy has graduated more than 45,000 people in the past decade. He serves as a global consultant and mentor to hundreds of CEOs and their aspiring leadership teams worldwide. Dr. Sam holds a Master of Arts in Leadership Studies and a Doctorate in Strategic Leadership. As the CEO of Sam Adeyemi GLC, Inc., Sam's mission is to raise awareness and high-impact leaders by unleashing untapped potential and seeing through broken facades to touch the hearts and minds of humanity. He is a prolific writer and has authored articles for Forbes.com and *The Agenda,* the online magazine of the World Economic Forum.

He is a member of the International Leadership Association and the Association of Talent Developers. He is married to Nike Adeyemi, a global speaker and social entrepreneur, and they are blessed with adult children.

Sam and Nike founded a church in Nigeria, the Daystar Christian Centre, that now reaches millions around the world.

RESOURCES FROM DR. SAM

CONNECT WITH DR. SAM

Info@SamAdeyemiGLC.com

SamAdeyemi.com

Dr. Sam Adeyemi

@sam_adeyemi

SamAdeyemi

@TheSamAdeyemi

Sam Adeyemi TV

IAmSamAdeyemi

Leadership Certification Program

To learn more about Dr. Sam's Leadership Certification Program availability and fees, contact David Ayodele:

Info@samadeyemi.com

Inside or Outside the United States, call 1-404-937-4911

SamAdeyemi.com

Media Press Kit

To review Dr. Sam's electronic media press kit, contact David Ayodele:

Info@samadeyemi.com

Inside or Outside the United States, call 1-404-937-4911

SamAdeyemi.com

Keynotes and Training

- Dear Leader
- Personal Transformation
- How To Become a Strategic Leader
- Leadership Certification Program

For availability, contact David Ayodele:

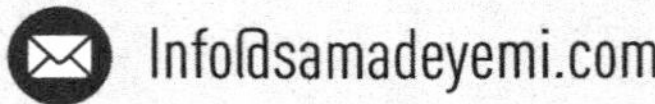

Info@samadeyemi.com

Inside or Outside the United States, call 1-404-937-4911

SamAdeyemi.com

ALSO BY DR. SAM

The following books are available on Amazon or your favorite online book retailer.

Customized signed books are available from the author.
Visit SamAdeyemi.com for more information.

Made in the USA
Middletown, DE
26 September 2023